AFRICAN WRITERS

Kenya, Cameroon, Nigeria, Côte d'Ivore, Burkina Faso,
Angola, Uganda, South Africa

A Journey in Writing

Media Associates International

AFRICA

African Writers: A Journey in Writing
Copyright © 2019 by Media Associates International

Published 2019 by

Media Associates International – Africa
PO Box 30446 GPO-00100
Nairobi, Kenya
mai–africa@littworld.org
www.littworld.org

ISBN 978-0-9799170-7-3

All rights reserved. No part of this publication may be reproduced, stored in a retrieval system, or transmitted in any form or by any means — electronic, mechanical, photocopy, recording, or any other — except for brief quotations in printed reviews, without the prior permission of the appropriate publisher.

"Little by little, it dawned on me. This flair for writing, this interest to string words together to communicate meaningful ideas, is more than a hobby: it is a mission with a vision, which makes it a calling."

Lawrence Darmani, Ghana
Award-winning author and MAI-Africa Trustee

Contents

Foreword	7
Buma Kor	9
Claude Preka Toty	19
Jennifer Karina	25
Joanna Ilboudo	33
Joel Sérgio	41
Lekan Otufodunrin	47
Lillian Tindyebwa	55
Pusonnam Yiri	63
Solomon Andria	71
Stella Chika Okoronkwo	79
Joan Campbell	89

Foreword

Collections bringing together writers from diverse nations and backgrounds to chronicle their rich and varied journeys have become somewhat of an MAI tradition. Africa was privileged to partake in this tradition for the first time over twenty years ago when the first edition of the Author Journeys book containing essays from African Christian writers was published.

A lot has changed since.

MAI has blossomed into a deeply impactful global ministry providing training in the hard places of the world so that the Church can satisfy the global hunger for the written word. As part of its growth journey, MAI has successfully planted MAI-Asia and MAI-Africa to hold in trust and advance the vision of MAI on these two continents. And while these exciting events have been taking place, a new crop of writers has emerged, seeking to use their gifts to the glory of God.

It is a fitting time, then, for this second collection of author journeys from Africa. It features writers from Cameroon, Côte d'Ivoire, Nigeria, Angola, Kenya, Burkina Faso, Uganda, and South Africa.

You will discover many gems hidden in plain sight in the pages of thisbook, among them:

Foreword

- What inspired Lekan Otufondunrin, former online editor at one of Nigeria's largest newspapers, to stay centred on God as he practiced his craft in a secular context.

- The story of the Barnabases that God brought into Stella Okoronkwo's life to help her along in her journey to become the best writer she could possibly be.

- How a childhood encounter with a library at a missionary school in Burkina Faso made a deep impression on Joanna Ilboudo and set her on a path that led her to writing.

I thank God for the men and women from across Africa who have contributed to this anthology, for the stories they are living and the stories they are telling. May the Church in Africa be nourished as a result of their obedience to God in using the thing that is in their hand.

I thank God also for those who have worked tirelessly and steadily behind the scenes to midwife this book, key among them being Lekan Otufondunrin, the editor, and Rose Birenge, the current chair of MAI-Africa. Our God creates his people in different flavours. Lekan and Rose are of a particular solid, faithful, dependable kind. They bless and steady everything with which they come in contact with a quiet but strong behind-the-scenes energy. This book would not have seen the printer's ink without them.

I pray that the journeys they share in this anthology will inspire you, challenge you, and ignite in you a vision to be a part of what God is doing through MAI to equip the Church in Africa so that it can transform individuals, societies, and nations through the power of the written word.

Wambura Kimunyu
Founding Chair, MAI-Africa

Buma Kor

Cameroon

Sir Buma Kor Dickson, 70, is a publisher, editor, writer trainer, and book development consultant in Yaounde, Cameroon. He received his training in Nigeria under the well-known Christian publisher Modupe Oduyoye of Daystar Press, Ibadan, along with further studies in publishing, management, theology, journalism, and communication skills within Cameroon and abroad (USA and UK). He publishes in English and in French, both general market and Christian books (meditations, literature for young adults, and some carefully selected people-oriented scholarly works. He is a visiting lecturer in communication at the Advanced School of Mass Communication, University of Yaounde II, and the Cameroon Christian University, Bali-Bamenda.

Sir Buma Kor has been a regular preacher of the Presbyterian Church in Cameroon (PCC) and freelance writer-columnist for some local and foreign media. He has published several articles and books, including *Searchlight: Poems* (1973), *Revival Palaver* in Bastos (1993), and *Thinking Aloud* (2011), a compendium of articles on various topics expressing an absolute need for a new Cameroon society. Among other awards, he was recently honoured with the Cameroon National Order of Valour (Chevalier de l'Ordre de Valeur). He is the current vice-president of the Copyright Corporation in Cameroon (SOCILADRA).

Over the years he has conducted writers' workshops around the country and alongside Isaac Phiri, formerly of Cook Communications, Adulaye Songo of CETCA, Côte d'Ivoire, Larry Brooks, and Bridget Impey. He has also organised training workshops for writers and/or publishers in different parts of Africa. He attended the Cook Communications Institute in Colorado Springs in 1996 and the APNET Trainer's Workshop in Accra, Ghana, in 1995. He was an active APNET trainer in different aspects of the book industry.

Finding the Desire of My Soul

I never thought I would be a writer someday. As I grew up in the seaside city of Victoria in southwestern Cameroon, now renamed Limbé, with its cool evening breeze and well-kept streets, my dream was to be an accountant. And so my father sent me to high school in Kumba, ninety-one kilometres away from Victoria, where I took business studies classes. It was not until I was in my fifth year, studying for the London School Certificate, that the gift of writing sprang up in the fertile soil of my open heart.

I loved reading poems and being carried away by the fancy of a poet's imagination. I copied almost all the poems in our English textbook into my notebook and enjoyed reading them to myself several times over at prep time: Robert Frost's *The Road Not Taken*, Longfellow's *A Psalm of Life*, and Wordsworth's *The Solitary Reaper*.

At day break I would recite some of the poems I had copied to my friends, reading and emphasizing some words and making gestures as if I were the poet. My friends did not know what was happening to me. I too did not know what was taking shape in me at a time when, instead of studying for my school certificate exams, I was carried away by some ancient poet to the land of his imagination. One day after morning classes, I retreated for solitude into some untrimmed bush near the school, foregoing the *garri* (cassava flakes) which, soaked in water to form a paste-like porridge, was our standard lunch. As I sat under the shade of a broad-leafed palm tree away from the scorching Kumba heat and the noisy students, I busied myself mimicking the style of one of the poems I had copied into my notebook, using it as a template to write my own poem in my own words. It was Longfellow's *Song of Hiawatha*.

> *Thus departed Hiawatha*
> *Hiawatha the Beloved*
> *In the glory of the sunset*
> *In the purple mists of evening*
> *To the regions of the home-wind...*

A copy-cat I was, even though I did not know this was the way of many a beginning poet. I started writing in the style of the English poets, in metres and pentameters, in rhymes and alliterations and stanzas of four alternate lines that rhymed at the end. What a new fancy I found and indulged in, taking up most of my study time.

Longfellow's *Song of Hiawatha* clearly inspired one of my earliest poems, *The Elegy of Formukong*, which reads in part:

> *Oh! Dying a youth in loathsome years*
> *Leaving treasures, friends, and dears*
> *Singing and mourning his departed soul...*

Without my knowledge, one of my friends took my poems to our English teacher, Mr. E. E. Ebiama, or as he was popularly known, "Ebiama of the World". He had earned this moniker because he was a talented man who at times behaved as if he was not fine "upstairs", bragging incessantly about his knowledge.

Ebiama of the World was a man of average height, slim and dark, nondescript in appearance but quite eccentric in manner. He moved in delicate steps as if he would fall. He would carry his transistor radio to the football field during matches, creating a spectacle, drawing attention to himself and away from the football match.

He was at first known as "Ebiama of Africa", but as his fame grew wild and spread like fire in the dry season, his name changed to "Ebiama of the World".

This was my English teacher—full of himself and confident. I was surprised that he had the humility to read my poems and comment on them.

Our school, which had the distinction of being the national high school, was in Kumba, in the southwest region of Cameroon. But it was not displayed proudly in front of the townspeople. Rather, it was hidden in some back street in a town

Finding the Desire of My Soul

known for its busy commerce and easy lifestyle. In later years, Kumba became known as "K Town" for reasons I do not care to tell. Reading on our own so as to follow the curriculum syllabus had become the order of most commercial colleges in those days. Clusters of students would steal away into the nearby bush to study from their textbooks instead of attending classes taught by mostly unqualified teachers. It was no surprise to us when, many years after we had left, the government closed the school. The surprise was that they had not closed it sooner.

Besides my foray into poetry, I had started writing essays as well, a skill I developed from studying the examples from our English textbook, *Certificate English* by Lancelot Oliphant. I was very good at writing essays. It came easily to me, and my English teacher was always happy with me. When my friend took my poems to my teacher, a new friendship developed between my English teacher and me.

One day, one of my essays appeared unexpectedly on the huge blackboard in our assembly hall. It was an essay I had written on our situation as students having to study in the bush instead of attending classes. I had titled it "The University in the Bush". My English teacher had corrected the essay, and a classmate with good handwriting had copied it on the assembly blackboard for all the students to read. It sparked fire among the students, and a debate raged between those who liked the article and those who did not. I wrote many more essays like this, and some of my poems were read by my fellow students.

I remember the day I first realized that I could become a writer. It was by all appearances an ordinary school day, just like any other if perhaps not as hot as you would find in Kumba during the dry season. The morning was progressing normally when I was called to the front of my classroom under the gaze of all my classmates to read a poem about our school, which I had written to celebrate its anniversary. Amidst thunderous applause, my English teacher, excited and proud of me, took me to see the proprietor with the poem I had written. There I was given a pat on the back and sent away with the picture stamped on my mind of myself as a successful writer someday. So an ordinary day was transformed into quite a special one.

I graduated from high school in 1968, in the month before the rainy season began, without attaining my full certificate. I had not obtained the required pass in the London School Certificate. I only had my books and the piles upon piles of poems I had written. I was now at home in my father's house in Victoria, which for reasons only politicians can provide, is known today as Limbé. My mother was not with us as she was always sick and had been taken to a healing home away from Victoria. I studied at home for the Ordinary Level GCE examinations.

Some of my former classmates were now employed by private businesses, pursuing our common dream of becoming accountants after graduation. We had had this idea of becoming chartered accountants after the likes of a Cameroonian in Nigeria we only knew as Mr. Njoh Litumbe, a chartered accountant with Akintola Williams & Associates. How phony it was! We would ruminate on our dreams, exercising them by drawing lines down imaginary figures and calculating their sums, like we figured an accountant would do with his "accounting stick".

I finally made my papers the following year, but I was not interested in writing the competitive exams that would have ushered me into the Public Service, as several of my friends had done. I wanted to become an accountant. I tendered applications for employment to many private companies. I guess I wrote over fifty applications to all sorts of business organisations or anything that looked like one, but none could offer me a position. I could not go to post-secondary school for the Advance Level GCE, and life became bitter and difficult. I would stay at home and cook for my father and myself. I remember how I would go to the market to buy provisions for the house and foodstuffs for the kitchen and carry them home in a jute bag on my head. Sometimes I would meet former schoolmates of the opposite sex. Ah-h! I would come home and ruminate and stare at the future.

My first job came without me writing an application. I was visiting a friend at a typing institute, and the proprietor, who had listened keenly to the explanations I gave my friend on how to type well, offered me a job teaching accounts and typing lessons. I worked there for some six months, during which I had the opportunity for the first time to type up a whole bunch of my own poems as well as some articles, which I sent to the newspapers. After working hours at my teaching job, I did volunteer work, typing letters and reports for my pastor, the Rev. Stephen Lyonga of the Presbyterian Church, Down Beach, Victoria, in his office. Rev. Lyonga introduced me to an expatriate worker with the Presbyterian Church, Mr. Gerhard Kauffman, for a real job in the treasury department of our church as a typist and bookkeeper.

Finding the Desire of My Soul

I met with Mr. Kauffman, a stoutly-built German with a well-trimmed moustache, in his air-conditioned and neatly organised office. He immediately gave me a test—a difficult text to type on a Hermes typewriter. The sound of my typing was like raindrops falling heavily on corrugated rooftops at the height of the rainy season. I made such an impression on the German that he hurriedly walked in from his office, briskly removed the sheet on which I was typing, and returned swiftly to his office. I thought I had done something wrong! The next thing I knew, he was calling other expatriate church workers to his office for a meeting. After that, I was employed.

At that time, the Presbyterian treasury department shared a compound at Down Beach with the Presbyterian Book Depot, which sold Christian books, general books, textbooks, stationery, and side-line articles. The Book Depot had several agencies in all the main towns of what was then West Cameroon, with the Victoria shop as the head office and main bookshop.

While working for the treasury department, I continued to write freelance for the newspapers and cultivated anew a habit from my secondary school days—reading.

One lunch hour without knowing why I was going there, I found myself in the Presbyterian bookshop just next door to my office, savouring the whole range of titles in the African Writers Series. The series, which I had first become aware of about the time I was graduating from secondary school in 1968, had by now published many titles, including *Things Fall Apart* by Chinua Achebe. I could not resist grabbing that title and by the end of the night had read the greater part of it. I devoured title after title until I had read all the books in the series. As I read these books, I studied their styles and looked forward with excitement and expectation to the next book in the series.

It was then that my writing began to change for the better. I had also learned by now about free verse in poetry, so I started writing "African" poetry without bothering about pentameters and solid rhymes. It was like a new birth. I found a treasure I knew I liked, and I plunged myself into it profusely. "The Mind to Answer" was among the first poems resulting from my rebirth.

When I was called
I was up on the roof
Mending the thatch over my house
The house within my lot
Exposed to no other
But myself.
As the call came
Breaking bounds and bonds
Tearing through sites and tides
I was up there on the roof
Working hard and unable to answer.
With the blowing of the cyclone
I tumbled to my knees
Grasping the puzzle of the exercise!
So different seemed the concept
So tempting the duty that
I shall learn to answer
To respond to wisdom
When next I am called.

I was on a roll. A prominent local newspaper, *Cameroon Chronicles,* was the first to publish one of my poems. Edward Blishen of the BBC read my poem "African Africanism", and *Présence Africaine* in France published some poems. I published news and feature articles in *Kamerun Times* and *Cameroon Outlook.* I also reviewed stories and poems in *Fako Magazine.*

I realized I could not go on like this. I had to take writing seriously. Reading through *A Book of African Verse* (Ed) and Christopher Okigbo's *Labyrinths,* I thought I needed to learn what made these poets write as effectively as they did. I had enrolled earlier with Rapid Results College (RRC) in London for my "A" Levels and knew about the courses offered by the Regent Institute, also in London. Now without hesitation, I registered for a course in journalism and creative writing with the Regent Institute, concurrently with those I was taking with the RRC.

Finding the Desire of My Soul

I continued working for the Presbyterian treasury department and soon became an assistant to the expatriate worker who served as treasurer for the PCC church schools. After some time, I was promoted to the post of cashier, keeping the moneys of the entire church brought to the treasury by the pastors.

My income was much better now, and I could easily pay for my tuition in both institutions. As my work load increased, my articles in the local secular presses decreased. By some twist of circumstances, the German expatriate workers in my office introduced me to Reverend Kappus, the topmost communications officer of our church radio and magazine production services, who had come to give the accounts of his department to the treasury department. He took me on as a stringer for the *Presbyterian Messenger*, and I often helped him produce the daily meditations and radio programmes, broadcast through the network of Radio Cameroon, Buea.

Reverend Kappus trained me on the job, and with the study materials I received from Regent Institute, I was able to make sense of what I was doing. The slippery roads I used to pass through in writing an article became smoother, and the high hills I would encounter each time I wrote a poem or prose started melting before I knew there were difficulties. Training was important, and I sought it at any cost.

One afternoon, in dire need of a mentor, I stumbled on *Adventure with a Pen* by Joyce Chaplin in the Presbyterian Book Depot. This book brought Christian writing into my life. As my writing improved, Reverend Kappus introduced me to Bengt Simonsson of the Africa Literature Centre, Kitwe, Zambia, and I became a correspondent for the Christian Writers Fellowship of Africa. As one thing led to another, Mr. Simonsson also introduced me to Donald Banks of the African Christian Press (ACP), Accra, Ghana, to whom I sent a collection of my sermons for publication. But Mr. Banks had no pity on me! I never got published by ACP.

I encountered Simonsson again as a textbook (*The Way of the Word: A Guide for Christian Literature Workers*) as I was studying for my theological formation at Immanuel College of Theology, Ibadan, Nigeria. I had gone there to study Christian literature and theology at the beginning of January 1973. I made it to Nigeria from Cameroon over a dastardly, dusty road, especially from Mamfe to the border town at Ekok. By then I knew my accounting days were over, and I was embracing a new love.

Nigeria is very different from Cameroon. Everything there is brisk, and money counts. After crossing the eastern region of the Igbos and the Effiks, I began a new life in the Yoruba city of Ibadan in western Nigeria. For reasons unexplained to me, Cameroonians in Nigeria were known as Biafrans by some people, about which some of my Yoruba schoolmates joked with me.

As I said, I bid goodbye to accounting the day I was admitted to study theology and publishing. I was trained henceforth to become a pastor, not of the spoken word, but of the written word. That changed my perspective entirely—my writing, my preaching, and my future career. My supervisor in publishing was Modupe Oduyoye, the venerated Nigerian Christian publisher and director of Daystar Press, Nigeria, where I was an intern. Mr. Oduyoye shaped me into a skilful editor and responsible publisher. It was he who introduced me to the business of Christian publishing, and all of a sudden, all my business lessons in high school became useful again.

Publishing is a multifaceted discipline. My studies in theology equipped me to edit and publish Christian books, an accomplishment that satisfied the desire of my soul. I had found the missing part of myself that fulfilled my yearning to become a useful person in my community. It fit well with my past activities, and my future was in sight.

My Christian faith, coupled with my theological formation, bolstered my writing as I came across a lot of books by different Christian writers from all over the world. In theological school, I read C. S. Lewis, Watchman Nee, Norman Vincent Peale, and a host of others. I learned to recognize good Christian writing from different perspectives—with the eye of an editor-publisher and with a desire to write for the Lord like an expert craftsman as these writers did.

In everything I write, I am conscious of my Christian stand. Now, whether I am writing a Christian book or an article for a secular press, the Christian viewpoint permeates every page.

In all the aforementioned, I thank the Almighty Lord for the gift of writing and for giving me a place in his vineyard to serve him and his people.

Preka Toty

Côte d'Ivoire

Claude Preka Toty is an economist with an MBA attained in Worms, Germany. His other achievements include project/programme management, Fair Trade USA Lead Certification trainer for the country of Côte d'Ivoire, and consultant in coaching/organisation development, management conflict facilitation and social enterprise responsibility. He is proficient in French, German, English, and three Ivorian languages.

Writing for the World

In 1984, after I had worked one year as a French and English teacher in Botro, a small town in the centre of Côte d'Ivoire, I decided to continue my studies. I think teaching is a good way to multiply and share knowledge, but for me teaching was a temporary job—one that enabled me to earn the means to study economics. I wanted to contribute to the development of my country. Something gave me the strength to believe that I could study again and expand my experience.

So with all my salary paid, I decided to fly to Europe. At that moment, I had no clear idea what I would do, but one thing was sure—I had to go.

My first stop was France, where my sister lived and where I could study in French. At the time, I believed that I could only study in French, which limited my options. Very soon, however, I realised that this was not the country where I wanted to study. I went to Italy, then to Belgium, hoping to find a better study environment. But I was still dissatisfied, so I went back to France.

One night I prayed, "Dear God, let me know my way because I do not want to be a tourist in Europe. You know I really want to study. Show me the way, *your* way."

A few minutes later, I heard clearly the word *"Mainz"*. But I did not know what that meant.

"What is Mainz?" I asked. The response came, "Go to the train station and ask there."

I obeyed. Upon inquiring at the train station, I learnt that Mainz is a city in what was then West Germany before the tearing down of the Berlin Wall and the reunification of East and West Germany. I purchased a ticket at 6:15 pm for a train that was leaving at 11:00 pm, then headed home to get my bag and return to the station.

My brother-in-law, with whom I was living, inquired where I was going so late in the night. I simply told him I was going to Mainz. He was quite anxious at my response and expressed it clearly since he knew nothing about Mainz.

"Where is Mainz?" he asked.

"I do not know," I replied.

"Be careful," was all he could say before I left.

That is how I travelled to West Germany, a country I had never visited before and where I knew no one. Nor did I have knowledge of a single word of German. But God allowed everything to go as smoothly as a well-working watch, and I started my studies there. I had to learn German before I could begin studying economics. I did this successfully, then studied economics with a focus on business administration and international development at Mainz University and at Worms Fachhocschule, a university in the city of Worms, Germany.

I was alone and thirsty, so I started to read the Bible. In fact, I would say that I "drank" every word with pleasure. Then one day I met a friend who worked in a university library. I asked her for some Christian books. She was happy to help me and offered me many books. This is how I came to read the writings of a Chinese author by the name of Watchman Nee. I read almost every book that Watchman Nee had written. As I was reading his books, it became clear to me that I had come to Germany for that mission: to write for the world!

Interestingly, the movable-type printing press was invented in Mainz, and the first books printed using movable type were manufactured in Mainz in the early 1450s.

When I was reading Nee's books, the message resonated so clearly that it seemed as though I myself was writing. This was very unusual because I did not have a background in writing or a particular gift for writing when I was growing up. But from the moment I started to read Nee, it felt as though he had just recently written the words I was reading and that I was being called to continue his writing. This despite the fact that Watchman Nee's writings had actually first been published many decades earlier in 1922.

Still, I took no action at this time to begin writing. I got married two years before I completed my studies, and after my studies I was busy trying to find a job. I returned home and began working. Ten years went by, and I had taken no action on my calling to write.

Writing for the World

Then I lost my job.

After I lost my job, my wife was often anxious about our future and became very nervous. Peace was gone from our lives. At this difficult time, I realised that a voice was speaking to me, but nobody else could hear it. One evening, I sat before my computer in my bedroom and I started to write for the first time.

The first book I wrote was a Christian crosswords book, which I showed to a pastor. He was amazed and asked if I had studied at a theological school. I told him I had not and inquired why he thought so. He responded by looking deep into my eyes and saying, "You are blessed."

I in turn was left amazed at his words. Then another friend of mine saw this small book and called a prophet. When the prophet saw me, he said, "God wants to make something of you as writer."

I was again amazed since I am an economist by training, so I just smiled at the words of these two Christian leaders. One of the puzzles in the crossword book was on the twelve tribes of Israel. After I had put them in a square so that they were bound together to form the puzzle, I realized that two of the tribes had been replaced. Through this exercise, the Lord revealed to me many secrets hidden in his Word. As a result, many people, most of them pastors, learnt God's Word easily.

After the crossword book, the "voice" told me to write another book. I obeyed, and this became a success. Then I wrote another book, which became a bestseller in Côte d'Ivoire, and a fourth book, which was read by many pastors. The books, which I wrote in French, were:

    1. *Jeux et mots croisés bibliques, n° 1 & 2*
    2. *L'or et l'argent appartiennent à Dieu*
    3. *Le mystère du nombre 666 révélé*
    4. *Le secret du tabernacle, Tome 1 & 2*

Sometimes a topic comes to me when I am rising in the morning, other times when taking a bath. But when it is time for me to write, it is like water pouring on my head, and I am neither physically thirsty nor hungry; I just write. When I am inspired, it takes me one or two weeks to complete a book.

I chose to self-publish because in Africa we do not have many publishing options. It is not easy being an African Christian writer because even if people like your books, African Christians do not read enough to encourage you. The money you invest to publish books does not always come back because there are not enough readers, and most of the time booksellers have difficulties paying your money back. For me, writing is a ministry, a passion. I will keep writing even if I cannot currently earn enough money from it.

Now, I am writing in a new form—to present God's Word through audio and video tools. I recently presented *The Tabernacle Secret Parts 1 & 2* successfully on a Christian radio show. I hope to continue to "write for the world" just as the "voice" told me that day in Germany.

Jennifer Karina

Kenya

Jennifer Karina is a psychologist, a certified professional coach, an Energy Leadership master practitioner, speaker, and author of the seminar series *Marriage Built to Last: After the Promise*, *Marriage Built to Last: Before the Promise*, *Marriage Built to Last: Healing beyond Betrayal*, as well as *Marriage Built to Last: The Companion Workbook*. Jennifer is a born-again Christian who engages her audience with passion and outstanding content, specializing in building authentic relationships in order to "Live, Love, and THRIVE". Jennifer is passionate about uplifting the lives of others and believes her purpose in life is to positively influence by stimulating, equipping, empowering, and encouraging individuals for better living. She is a thought leader in her area of influence and has been regularly featured on television and radio as well as in national newspapers. She is a sought-after speaker for seminars, conferences, and key-notes.

In 2015 in Mumbai, India, Jennifer was recipient of the World Women Leadership Award (WWLCA) in recognition of her valuable contribution to society and industry. She was also recognized for her achievement as East Africa's Regional Winner in the Welfare and Civil Society Organization Sector of CEO Global's Most Influential Women in Business and Government 2017 Awards. Jennifer holds a master of arts degree from Durham University, New Castle, UK, and is pursuing a PhD in Educational Psychology. She has attended professional courses from various institutes, including Cranfield School of Management, UK, Strathmore Business School, Kenya, and Harvard Business School, USA.

Jennifer has been married to Bob Karina for over forty years. She has three married children and several grandchildren. She enjoys spending quality time with her family, writing, travelling, swimming, and playing golf.

My Journey of Writing: Joys and Tribulations

In my high school days, they called me "Dear Dolly", in reference to the well-known advice column published in *Drum*, a popular South African English-language magazine, during the 1970s when I was a teenager. "Dolly" was an accomplished "agony aunt" who always had a word of advice for those who cared to write to her. I too responded to those in challenged relationships through letters in the mail. In the seventies we had no technology like today. Those whom I supported in this fashion have always been thankful and are so pleased to see that I finally pursued my passion and purpose. I must say that they called out my gift and God used me to minister to them.

I always enjoyed reading and writing and have always had a way with words. But I never saw myself as an author. On the other hand, I enjoyed teaching, mentoring, and counselling. Whenever I held various training sessions, time always spilled over to long hours with lingering individuals who did not want to go home as we continued to engage on the topic. I gave handouts for homework to get them to chew on good material while they were away, but it was not always enough. I was encouraged to write a book, but the hardest part was believing in myself and being confident enough to allow myself to stumble and fall in the process of learning a new skill.

My writing finally happened after an intense affliction and with much encouragement from my husband. I had so much pain and needed to express it the best way I knew how—by writing. I wrote as therapy and would destroy the material after I had written. Then one day a friend visited me when I had just completed some writing, which I shared.

"Oh my! This should be published," my friend remarked. "You surely have a gift for writing, and you should use it."

I decided to keep the writings, eventually showing them to a publisher. The publisher affirmed the value of what I'd written, saying I should consider writing a book on the topic of conflict resolution. I had not healed from my particular hurt, so I proceeded with much difficulty. Writing on the topic only seemed to aggravate the raw pain. I would write a lot, then delete the work. I wanted perfection, and I was falling short of my own expectations.

"Do I really have anything to offer?" I often asked myself. "Who would be interested in reading about conflict and conflict management written by a novice with little leadership or conflict management skills?"

Eventually I grew in confidence and shared the writing with another acquaintance, who offered me some excellent tips—including not to delete anything I wrote and to develop an outline for my work. Although I regretted having lost so much material, I was glad to realise that everything we put down on paper is important, if not for the immediate project, perhaps for another one in the future.

I must admit that the hardest part of writing is identifying the right topic. I eventually settled on a topic I was well conversant with—marriage—and included a chapter on conflict management. I discovered it is so much easier to write on a topic with which I am conversant.

The title of my book became a reality after several months of searching, seeking, and trying many titles before I decided on *Marriage Built to Last: After the Promise*. When the book was finally published, everyone, including my family, was excited about it. That is, everyone but me! I was anxious and afraid. I was about to expose my ignorance and foolishness to the world, so I thought, opening myself to criticism, insult, and abuse. I had just seen a book review in the daily newspapers that had really bashed an author, denting the author's image greatly. The book was said to be shallow, to display a poor command of the English language, and to have too many spelling mistakes. Wow! I was afraid of getting a similar bashing. I was afraid of releasing the book into the market. I was even ready to absorb the loss and simply let that pass.

"What was I thinking?" I berated myself. "I am not an authority on the subject."

I was also afraid because I had shared some personal information about which I began to feel uncomfortable. I was afraid that I might have some language and spelling errors. In summary, I was afraid of the unknown. I put the books in a basement. Two months later, I was still not ready to begin distribution.

"Who will be interested in reading from me? Who am I anyway? I am not Hilary Clinton or Mother Teresa," I remember telling my publishing consultant, who prayed with me and gave me a scripture that opened not only my mind, but my doors: "No eye has seen, no ear has heard, no mind has conceived what God has prepared for those who love him" (1 Corinthians 2:9).

My consultant assured me that no book starts off perfect and that any flaws would eventually be corrected as we printed additional copies. In the meantime, I should simply trust God, who was using me as a vessel of worth and had anointed me for the ministry of marriage and relationships. For those God calls, he anoints and gives them GRACE for the appointment. I obliged, and the rest is history. My close friends and mentors came together and prayed with me. I dedicated the book at my church, and with the anointing of God, was happy to release the book to the market. It received an overwhelmingly positive response. The book has empowered many individuals, and I continue to receive testimonies on a daily basis from those it has helped.

A Difficult Journey

The reason I chose self-publishing was that my book had still not been published by a traditional publisher even after waiting for over two years. I was continuously reminded that there were many other books to be published and mine would have to wait a while. The interpretation I took from this scenario was that my book was not worthy of readers, and for that reason there were better books that took priority. This negatively impacted my self-esteem and self-image.

However, my dream to see my book published was prompting me on a daily basis, and I realized I had to do it, even if it meant investing my own funds to have my book published. I knew I had a compelling story that needed to be told. Too many people were suffering in their relationships, and I knew I could help them thrive. That inspired me to go ahead with self-publishing.

Self-publishing also meant that I owned all rights to my book and was responsible for the distribution. I must admit this was a tall order, a major challenge, since I had no experience or knowledge of book distribution and I was depending on my friends and family to sell the book. The price that I'd set for my book was also on the high side.

"Your book cannot sell at that price," I was told repeatedly. "Drop it to half that price, and then you will sell."

But I had invested so much in the book that I did not wish to sell it for less. Who were these people with absolutely no idea how much I'd invested in this book to tell me the price at which I should sell it? Bookstores were not interested either. They would ask me to leave a sample, but despite several follow-up phone calls enquiring whether they were ready to place an order, they would just keep telling me to wait.

My publishing consultant explained to me that book sales would depend entirely on my personal marketing skills through various speaking engagements and promotions and that the book would sell only if I had visibility and impact. It was clear to me that the sole responsibility was mine.

This was all an unfamiliar journey since I had never marketed books before, and I found myself battling fear. I searched for a distributor long and hard without any success. I was a brand-new author, so nobody took me seriously. They did not care when I told them that I had a good product of significant value to help readers. The best I was able to do as far as distribution was finding a small bookshop willing to accept my books on a consignment basis. In return, I promised that I would refer customers to them.

After feelings of failure, rejection, and dejection, I finally collected myself. Surprisingly, those from whom I had expected support did not rise to the occasion. How that hurt! Instead, they discouraged me totally. It was a difficult journey. The only thing that kept me going was something within me that prompted me, urged me, "You can do it; press on!" This is called passion. I finally gathered courage and a good attitude towards my book and decided to bite the bullet. After all, I had written a powerful book. If I did not believe in it, who would? I had what it took—knowledge, wisdom, understanding, and mastery of the topic. That was the beginning of greater things.

My Journey of Writing: Joys and Tribulations

Owning My Book

From then on, I owned my book, believed in it, and spoke about it everywhere I went. Rather than asking friends to sell the book for me, I sought opportunities to speak at their churches. Whenever I introduce myself, I always take the opportunity to let the audience know that I am the author of a great book—*Marriage Built to Last: After the Promise*.

Bookshops were also willing to let me sit in for a day to meet and greet their customers and talk about my book. This was powerful. The customers were happy to have an autographed copy, and they felt privileged to have my attention.

"You are so passionate about your topic," many often responded.

Oh yes, I am. I want to make a difference in the institution of marriage, and I am a declared ambassador of the institution. My brand slogan is *Marriage Built to Last*. That is my identity, and most people know me through my brand. I did not purpose that as the brand, but after my book launch the media picked it up. And because of the reporting in both print and digital media, it stuck. It is important to remain with the brand by which people identify you.

My message is clear. It is about building a marriage that lasts. I have been married for over thirty years. I have adult children who are now married, and I am enjoying several grandchildren. When I speak on the topic of marriage, I am an authority because I have lived it—and exceptionally well, for that matter. I have researched extensively on this subject, and gradually I was branded and even given the title "Dr. Karina—the Guru of Relationships". I discovered that it is not until you like and believe in your work that others will admire and trust it as well. I have caused a revolution in the area of marriage and relationships simply because I am crazy about the topic and writing about it.

Before my book was ready, my vision was to see every family live, love, and thrive. I desired that every Kenyan family would have the book and that every other African country would come to realise they too needed it. Today the book is read all over the world through Amazon and other online bookstores. This is simply because I did not give up on my dream, my passion, my desire, but trusted God, who always seeks a faithful vessel willing to be used for his glory. I credit everything I do in ministry for the glory of God. I have no fear acknowledging that without God the work that I do would be in vain, for he is the author of the institution of marriage and the giver of every good and perfect gift.

To get the book sales moving, I strategically sought speaking opportunities, prepared well, and delivered effectively. Each opportunity would land me another one, and before long I had so many engagements I began to refer or decline. Initially I did it for free. Now I charge a fee for any speaking engagement, and they are happy to pay because I have created a brand. When I began passionately speaking on the topic of marriage and relationships, I approached churches and Christian organizations because they were easier for me to access. I approached the church pastors and women's leaders, asking them to grant me an opportunity to speak to their congregation. Today I receive invitations from both the public and private sector. I am a sought-after motivational speaker because of the book. I have a weekly newspaper column and a weekly show on radio and TV, simply because someone identified my gifting and passion for my topic.

A Meaningful Experience

When I embarked on my writing, I also pursued a master's degree in counselling psychology and continued to pursue various other professional courses that have helped towards my personal growth and development. I pursued these diligently so that people who choose to read my books know that I have invested time in seeking knowledge, and so that I can be respected in my area of specialization—family and marriage therapy. While it is alright to write a book through inspiration, credibility is higher when the author has credentials in the area of her expertise. Credentials also build trust and make marketing the book easier.

I always use my brand to sign off in my correspondence, which continues to be a way of marketing my book. Interestingly, those who see it for the first time always ask me about it. This gives me an opportunity to preach the gospel of marriage and relationships as God intended.

Building a website, creating a basic Facebook page, and opening a Twitter account have been new learning experiences for me. Being digital does not come naturally to me, yet I recognize it as a necessity. I receive messages from lots of people desiring to be supported, and I respond to each one of them. This takes a lot of time, and I must admit I am currently overwhelmed as I seek solutions. Social media is powerful, and its reach is very extensive. For no fee at all, you can reach out to the world and share your message. I began with sending a message once a week to all my fans, and the results were amazing—references, commendations, as well as great friendships. Connecting with fans is meaningful. People who believe in the brand become great ambassadors and will do well in spreading the word, even selling. You can even discuss a commission for every book that they sell.

In order to keep the customers engaged, from time to time I create a video of a section of the book as a teaser. This has served as a powerful promotional tool when it comes with the book as an offer. I use this every time I have a speaking engagement, and people buy with excitement because of the free DVD with the book. Their response gives me the strength to pursue my writing with passion. I do, however, recognize that it is now time to revise my original book *Marriage Built to Last* and add some interesting features.

I am currently creating two books: *Marriage Built to Last Workbook* and *Case Studies*. What I have found interesting is that my confidence is still challenged when I embark on new projects. Feelings of inadequacy still come, but what helps is keeping faithful to writing and maintaining a schedule. In the end, when someone else looks at the work and says, "Wow, this is great!", it is refreshing.

Despite the many challenges of writing, God is faithful. "Fear not for I am with you," he constantly comforts me. He also reminds me, "It is not always about you, it is about the bigger picture."

I thank God for finding me worthy of his calling. I am pressing on and looking forward to launching my two new books and creating a new edition of *Marriage Built to Last*. My prayer is that God will continue to use me through the gift of writing to touch the lives of people, young and old, to live lives pleasing to him and his purposes for his own glory!

Joanna Ilboudo

Burkina Faso

Joanna Ilboudo has been the founder and president of ACTS Ministry since 2005. She has experience in leadership and management as director of a radio station, developing, establishing, and managing seven different station locations over the span of twelve years.

Joanna received an award from Panos Institute for West African radio production excellence for a June 1997 programme on human rights. She has been the managing editor of the magazine and publishing house Contact Editions for more than twenty years. She has published and distributed AIDS awareness literature.

Joanna received a prize during the biannual cultural week, "Semaine Nationale de la Culture, SNC", in both 1986 and 1994 for short story writing and drama. She has also authored:

- *Pitié pour ma soeur !* (Pity for My Sister, a drama on FGM)
- *Au nom de la foi !* (short story on vulnerability of children)
- *Destinée via adversité*
- *Et si toute ma vie était louange*
- *Parcours de femmes* (life experiences of women in leadership in Burkina)

Circumstances, Talents and Open Doors

The Bible says the Lord called each of us from our mother's womb and has a destiny for us to fulfil. I know that for me circumstances, talents, and open doors guided me to find my destiny.

Change came to my life when I was attending my fourth new school since I had started primary school. We moved quite often because my father's job as a policeman required him to do so. Sometimes it was fun to live in different parts of the country, learn new dialects, and meet new friends. Nevertheless, it was very difficult on the family when we had to move in the middle of the school year. We weren't allowed to skip any school. My parents believed that all eleven of us children should go to school and that we should excel.

I will be forever grateful to my parents for encouraging me in my studies. Every child, no matter whether they are male or female, should be able to learn about the world, the things around them, and the God who loves them. They need to understand that they are precious and that the Lord has a plan for their lives.

The year was 1971 when my father decided to enrol us in a boarding school run by French missionaries so we would not be uprooted from school each time we moved. For the first time in my life, I discovered a library. I had never before seen a room with so many books. Amazed, I began to look at the books one by one. I read all the book titles and then looked inside each one. Never before had I imagined I would see so many different types of books. Never having had an opportunity to choose from so many, I first picked books with many pictures. The series called *Tintin* was my first choice. After finishing that series, I couldn't stop reading. *Alice in Wonderland, Snow White, Beauty and the Beast, Cinderella*—I found them all so interesting. I loved the different styles of writing.

In my last year of primary school, my teacher, Mr. Dennis Oubida, instituted a writing competition for the class. Each month he assigned us to write a story to be read in front of the class. We critiqued each other's writing, and the best stories were hand-copied in a special notebook kept by our teacher. We dipped our pens in the ink wells to write. We didn't have ballpoint pens or computers in those days.

When it was time to go to secondary school, I attended a boarding school for girls called the Collège de Jeunes Filles de Loumbila. To my great surprise and pleasure, this school had even more books to read. The missionary instructors devoted themselves to teaching us proper French. Reading texts aloud in class created images in my mind. Books by Honoré de Balzac and poems by Verlaine and Victor Hugo inspired me to write.

At this time, I discovered a series by Swiss writer Madeleine Secretan that included such titles as *Hugo and Billy*, *Mario the Child of the South*, and *Oliver My Nephew*. I had the joy of reading these books, but they also shaped my spiritual life. The stories of teenagers told in these books were good examples for me in my Christian walk.

The books I read impacted my life so deeply that when I grew up and had children, I made sure they read them too. I scrimped and saved to buy good children's books. I bought them when my own kids were growing up, and they all read them. Books and the truths imparted through the stories made a difference in my children's lives. The books still reside proudly on my bookshelves at home.

After secondary boarding school, I went on to high school at the Catholic school in Ouagadougou. There I was destined to enter another phase of my life. I experienced disappointment. I was good at science, and my thought was to study medicine. But the high school I was assigned to did not prepare students for a career in medicine. Instead, its **programme** was structured toward a career in literature. I was not allowed to change my course of study because I had a scholarship to this school that would be forfeited if I left. With eleven children to support, my parents couldn't afford to pay my fees at another school, so I was obliged to stay. This was very hard for me. For the first three months, I cried almost every day and was depressed. I enjoyed literature and writing, but I thought I wanted a career in medicine.

The Bible says that man plans his way, but the Lord directs his steps. Sometimes the Lord will gently guide us in his way for our lives. If we allow ourselves to be

Circumstances, Talents and Open Doors

open and teachable, we will find it. Faced with the impossible, I resigned myself to my fate. For a while I became an introvert and spent more time alone. It was during this time of transition that I began to write poems. I remembered the great poems of Verlaine and Victor Hugo. Looking back at that time of focusing on writing, I can see the benefits of the experience. Instead of being outgoing and having fun times with friends, I was developing my writing gift. I tend to drive myself to excel, but there were other lessons to learn while being more meditative. I set goals for myself, followed them to completion, and then set more.

Recently, a leader of my country came to a ceremony I had organized and observed, "You never do small things; you always try to do over and above what everyone else would do in the same place." Today, when I have a project, I try to avoid distractions and focus on what is most important for me and the work I am doing. For this reason, while travelling I tend to avoid most tourist attractions. I'd much rather take the free travel time to read new books discovered along my journeys. I can enjoy staying in my room for an entire weekend in order to meet my reading and writing goals.

The Lord has given each one of us different talents and anointing. It is up to us to figure out how to use them to bring him honour and glory. It has been said that "your gift will make room for you". Gifts given by God will open doors of opportunity for you when used in his way.

For me, this introverted or contemplative attitude opened doors in the area of my writing. Writing is work. It takes time to concentrate and put your ideas on the page. This focus on writing doesn't cause me to avoid people. I do like to connect with one person or small groups and make all efforts for these relationships to be meaningful and deep. I hate superficial ones. What a waste!

Don't waste your talents by using them in meaningless pursuits. Find a way to use them to help others. I come from a country where there is much suffering. Women and children are the ones most affected by poverty and abuse. No one knows the pain another binds up in her heart. Poems echo the heart pain, showing the sufferer that her suffering is understood and that she is not alone.

I wrote a poem about this pain. Pain that no one else knows because it dwells in silence.

Joanna Ilboudo

The silence of the heart

When the hands are moving and feet tremble,
The heart in silence speaks in the quiet of the night!
When the eyes fill with mists and the body shivers,
The heart in silence speaks in the quiet of the night!
Do you hear the silence of the heart?
He says what the shivering body feels,
It expresses what the hands, the feet are suffering!
Do you understand the silence of the heart in the quiet of the night?
Look at the lost eyes,
Observe the hands, the warm feet,
Touch the moist body,
The buried head!
When the heart in silence speaks in the quiet of the night,
Only the heart can understand!

Between 1978 and 1982, I wrote more than a dozen poems. My linguistics professor at the University of Ouagadougou in Burkina Faso liked my poems. He took them to be published in a local newspaper but unfortunately lost them. We did not have computers to save copies of documents in those days.

I think that the Lord wanted me to move ahead and not concentrate on past victories. He had new things for me to do that needed developing.

It "just so happened" that the government of Burkina Faso initiated a way to promote local writing and encourage young writers. In 1986 they launched a national-level writing competition. I entered and won a prize! This was a great encouragement to me.

My submission for the competition was a drama based on memories from my own life as a girl growing up in a village. The drama concerned a family who decided to send their girls for Female Genital Mutilation (FGM).

Circumstances, Talents and Open Doors

FGM is an accepted evil tradition in Burkina Faso. I remember my shock when I saw parents who were educated or held high public positions in the city forcing female circumcision on their daughters. As a young girl, I tried to convince them by telling them that my father was against the practice. He would never permit circumcision for me or my sisters. Unfortunately, at that time I was not qualified to dissuade the other parents from their plan, and the girls were circumcised. The memory remained vivid in my mind. When I had the opportunity to tell that story in a written format and as a drama, I used it.

Writing can address current issues of our day. Writers can transform lives using the gift God has given them. He will give you opportunities to stand for righteousness.

Later in 1992, I entered another competition and won another prize. This second story was about children who were beggars in the city. I became acquainted with them as they passed regularly by my home, and I learnt their sad stories. They scavenged for food in the streets of the capital city, Ouagadougou.

One day one of the children was so hungry that he ate spoiled meat and died a painful death. After hearing this tragic story, I decided to use my writing to encourage parents to educate their children or to get them professional training instead of sending them out to beg or hunt for food on the street. Struggling to survive on the street does not give a child hope for the future. Each child has a right to find his own destiny.

Through these writing projects, the Holy Spirit showed me that writing is a ministry. The Holy Spirit clearly showed me that I could serve the Lord with my pen. I was overjoyed. I rejoiced at the knowledge that writing was a ministry. I stopped wondering how I could serve the Lord. This was a way I could serve the Lord as a woman. I attended Bible school in England, knowing that women are not allowed to preach in churches in my country.

I had a growing desire to fill the void in the area of writing among evangelicals. I launched *Contact* magazine for older teens and adults. Besides publishing the magazine, I also trained some budding writers and exhorted others about the need for Christians to write. Today, I tell everyone to consider writing as a powerful ministry to expand the Lord's Kingdom.

Joanna Ilboudo

My introduction to Media Associates International (MAI) and its LittWorld conferences gave me confidence and widened my vision for literature. MAI encouraged me in the publishing of *Contact* magazine. The opportunity to meet people from around the world with the same thirst for writing encouraged me to persevere in my writing despite the challenges of gender and isolation. The consecration and diligence of MAI leaders as well as that of other publishers and writers have given me strength along the way.

In the past few years, I have published books that deal with spiritual growth and encourage readers to consider the avenues of praise and worship. These are two keys for believers as they develop closer communion with the Lord and win great battles in life.

Although I live in a context where people were slow to understand the importance of the written word, I do believe writing is an important tool for the Church. Early Christians like Paul and John reached hearts and transformed lives through the written word. They died long ago, but their writing lives today. Writing can be a powerful spiritual gift.

Young Christians who develop their writing gifts, follow the guidance of the Holy Spirit, and look for opportunities to use their talents will change their own lives and the lives of those who come after them.

Don't give up. Keep seeking the right path for your life. Ask the Lord to guide your way. Look for doors to open. If one closes, look for another. Those who ask, seek, and knock will find the door open to their destiny.

Joel Sérgio

Angola

Joel Sérgio is a Christian, teacher of Sunday biblical school, and author of four self-help books, including *You Too Can Succeed*, the first motivational book by an Angolan. Joel Sérgio is married to Yona Ermelinda. They have four children and live in Luanda, Angola.

When All Doors Close

In the late 1980s and early 1990s, a new wave was emerging among young people in Angola. They would find a way to travel to Europe, where they would apply for work on building construction sites. At that time, several countries were on the verge of joining the European Economic Community, so there was plenty of construction work. It was common to see adverts at the building sites seeking willing young immigrants to work, and the African immigrants seized the opportunity to earn some money, rebuild their lives, and help their families in Africa.

I aspired to be one of those guys. After a trip to Brazil in 1990, I considered Europe to be my next logical step. Some factors put me among those with a greater opportunity to emigrate successfully. My three older brothers had European citizenship and could therefore help by sending me an invitation to obtain the entry visa to a European country. In addition, my uncle, who was quite wealthy and in the Angolan army, could help with the tickets. Indeed, he had helped others in this way in the past, and I believed it would not cost him much to help me in what I had come to believe was the "project of my life."

Even so, I had a point against me: I suffered from epilepsy.

In the 1990s, Angolans commonly linked epilepsy to spiritual forces, and a great sense of mysticism surrounded the disease. Ignorance of about epilepsy, in particular the unconscious moments that followed an epileptic seizure, necessitated keeping myself and the fact that I suffered from this disease somewhat hidden. Epilepsy precluded me from military service. It was also the barrier that kept me away from my dream of going to Europe. While I cried for an invitation letter, my brothers feared the possibility of calamity. They were concerned that if I worked in construction, I ran the risk of suffering a crisis at the top of one of the buildings and perhaps dying.

I turned to the Lord, and I began to pray for my healing as well as for my trip. Unfortunately, the enthusiasm gradually waned, and disappointment took hold of me. How could there be a loving God on the one hand while on the other hand he did not heal me and would not help me travel? After all, all I wanted was to go to Europe in search of better living conditions! How could God be good if he did not allow me to travel in search of a better life? It is easy to close our eyes on God's will while we want him to do our will.

One day after my brothers had made it clear I could not depend on their help to travel, I ran to my church looking for someone to talk to, hoping for a word of encouragement or comfort. But everyone was too busy going from one meeting to another, and they could not listen to me. So I prayed for a special word from God at that moment. Opening my Bible randomly, I landed on Ezekiel 37 and read the prophet's vision of the valley of dry bones.

When I finished reading, I was very excited. God had shown me that he was able to accomplish his will for me. I no longer felt that he was far off or that he did not care enough to intervene in my life. I began to think that he, being so powerful, could have other plans for my life. For the first time ever, I felt that my life had some value to God.

I remained in Luanda and I started to reorganize my life. I started writing a film script, a crime detective story set in Italy. I believed it to be so good it would eventually become a movie. But the story was never published. Indeed looking at it years later, I felt ashamed of the poorly written text. Still, it served well as the beginning of my writing career. I also decided to go back to school to finish my college degree. In the struggle to emigrate, I had dropped out of school because the trip was always "very close to happening". As a result, I had been out of school for more than nine years.

Meanwhile, my passion for reading was increasing. I decided to accept an offer from Scripture Union to become an officer of the organization. I fulfilled several roles, working in the office as a receptionist, cleaning the office, organizing library books, responding to letters, and writing the minutes of our meetings. In the Scripture Union library, I had access to books such as *The Cross and the Switchblade* by David Wilkerson, which I liked because they gave me a new understanding of God using ordinary people to do great things.

At the time, my favourite book was *Lord, I've Got a Problem* by Don Baker because I still suffered from epilepsy and as a result was not well accepted in society. I did eventually receive the healing I was praying for, although it took several years and happened only when I had given up on going to Europe.

When All Doors Close

As I read more books, I also began to develop a unique taste for writing. Gradually, people around me were beginning to notice this talent in me. Without any training, I began writing gospel tracts. One of the tracts I wrote was *Cabaz de Natal* (*Christmas Basket*). This refers to a special basket containing typical foods eaten at Christmas—such as cod, reindeer potatoes, chickpeas, and sweet oil—that is distributed by families at Christmas time. In this booklet, I highlighted the similarity between this Christmas basket and the great offering that God made to men by sending his son.

Another tract I wrote was *Justiça Injusta?* (*Unfair Justice?*), which spoke of how God had sent us a just Man to die for the unrighteous so that they might be made the righteousness of God.

The two pamphlets were published by the evangelical bookstore O Barquinho and were distributed in the bookstore to churches that were looking for evangelistic materials.

Later I attended a workshop for writers organized by the communication department of the Evangelical Alliance of Angola. I have always been very attentive to the Portuguese language, correcting people who expressed themselves wrongly. I have very keen ears and attentive eyes to the artistry and grammar of the written word. After the workshop ended, I was invited to join a group of evangelical writers called Jango dos Escritores Evangélicos (Meeting of Evangelical Writers), which met on Saturdays. The communication department had created more than seven Jangos all over the country. In these meetings, we shared ideas and corrected each other's writings. Eventually I was asked to be the editor of our Jango in Luanda.

Through the efforts of the Jangos and the help of a Brazilian missionary, Hans Udo Fuchs, who belonged to an organization of Brazilian publishers that helped Angola with literature, some very good books were published. The first book from our Jango, written by one of our most talented authors, Sonia Gomes, was published. The book was a success. Sonia continued to write, published two more books, and joined the União dos Escritores Angolanos (Angolan Writers Union), which published five more of her books. Sonia Gomes is one of our most successful Angolan writers.

I, on the other hand, gave up writing to dedicate myself fully to my studies at the Catholic University of Angola, where I was studying production management and marketing. With my breach, the group disbanded. On the one hand, Sonia's success was an encouragement to the writers in our Jango. On the other hand, it generated some anxiety, leaving us to wonder when our own turn might come.

I continued my studies in appalling conditions, as there was no money for school fees, transportation, or learning materials. Some eight years later when I completed my studies, I returned to writing. I decided to write a book to encourage Angolan youth to fight for their dreams even if they lacked life's basic amenities. I wanted them to realise that they too could succeed in life if they would only cling to God and have a plan, a dream, commitment, continuous learning, humility, perseverance, and fear of the Lord. This book, *You Too Can Succeed: Seven Tips for You to Live at the Height of Your Dreams*, was published in September 2009.

My book completed, I encountered some difficulties. Some of my old teachers, classmates, and even friends would not read it. This discouraged but did not defeat me. Some of my friends did not accept the proposed price. They doubted my ability to write a book on success, therefore considered the price too high. Besides all this, there were difficulties with finances and distribution. I received suggestions to pay for the distribution, but I didn't like the idea, and even if I had wanted to, I had no money. I had run out of resources getting the book to Angola, as it had been produced in Portugal and printed in Brazil by Imprensa da Fé.

I have not sold all the copies of this book; I still have some at home, though not many, thanks to God. But the experience of publishing this book has been priceless. As a result, I got to know many people who had written books but did not know how to get them published. In addition, my book became a national symbol, as it was the first motivational book written by an Angolan author. Other books followed.

After I had published my first book, I attended the LittWorld workshop in Limuru, Kenya, where I learnt a lot from some famous and respected Christian authors, such as Jeanette Windle and Robin Jones Gunn. There I also had the opportunity to network and engage with some African colleagues with whom I still communicate. I was the only member coming from an African country where Portuguese is the official language.

When All Doors Close

In 2011, I published another book, this time as the co-author with a young woman. The book portrayed the correspondence between a young person recovering from drug addiction in a rehabilitation centre and a young lady finalist of the Miss Luanda contest. This book received a lot of publicity because all the staff at the Comité Miss Luanda were involved, and it was a success.

Applying all I had learnt at LittWorld about ghost-writing and co-authoring, I wrote and published two more books. Both were written with two of my brothers, one of them a dance teacher in Italy and the other an Olympic athlete who has left Europe and is now practicing beach volleyball in Angola.

In 2013, I founded a company called Tchi Criativa, which aims to publish books by national and international authors and meet the great need for publishing houses in Angola. The name Tchi Criativa roughly translates to "Publications of Love". We are working hard selling books produced in Brazil and in Portugal in order to raise funds to open the publishing house.

We have a long way to go towards getting relevant literature to the readers in Angola. Some books we have received from outside no longer provide answers to the challenges we face in Angola. For instance, one of the unique challenges the Church in Angola faces is whether to adopt a partisan stance now that the country has done away with the communist system. Another challenge is getting people to speak about Christ in partisan gatherings. One of our greatest challenges is finding the courage to debate human rights issues. While some of our challenges are similar to those faced by other countries, the context in Angola has changed somewhat, and we need books that challenge the Church to take a stand for Christ.

We believe that publishing national authors will contribute greatly in this effort and will grow our evangelical presence as "salt" and "light of the world". We look forward to helping Christians embrace their role in that transformation, not only in Angola, but also in Mozambique, São Tome, Guinea-Bissau, and Cape Verde, which are also Portuguese-speaking nations, as well as the rest of the world.

I have not forgotten, however, that all these doors were opened when all other doors closed to me.

Lekan Otufodunrin

Nigeria

Lekan Otufodunrin is a journalist and media career development specialist based in Lagos, Nigeria.

Otufodunrin is presently managing editor of online and special publications for *The Nation* newspaper. He was formerly Sunday editor of the paper as well as Group News editor of *The Punch* newspaper.

He is secretary of the Africa Region of the World Association for Christian Communication (WACC) and member of the board of trustees of Media Associates International (Africa). He is a fellow of Thomson Foundation, Cardiff, UK, Poynter Institute (School for Journalists), Florida, USA, and Africa Leadership Initiative (ALI) Media Programme. He is also founder of Journalists for Christ International Outreach.

Otufodunrin's books includes *Purpose-Driven Journalism, Excelling in Journalism, Reporter Extraordinaire, Journalism of My Life*, and *The Journalist You Ought to Be*.

Journalist for Christ

Due to his dad's inability to pay his school fees, my dad, Chief Adebisi Otufodunrin, didn't complete his high school studies. However, in the late 1960s while working as a clerk in a bookshop in Ibadan, he developed a great interest in reading books, especially the literary ones. As a result, he started the modest collections which I grew up with in our house.

My dad's books and heaps of daily newspapers sparked my interest in reading and writing. To keep me busy during my high school holidays, he would give me books to read and summarise. I tackled the assignments and voraciously read other story books, especially the Pacesetter short story series, which was written by African writers for an African audience. I relished titles such as *Evbu My Love*, *The Blackmailers*, and *Christmas in the City*. I started dreaming of writing my own versions. I eventually wrote my own short stories in my school notebooks, but I did not have the confidence to show them to anyone for fear of being told they were not good enough. I had no doubt, however, that someday I would be a published author.

In the daily newspapers—for which I sometimes had to go to newsstands to buy for my father when the vendors didn't show up on our own street early enough—I enjoyed reading columnists such as Seyi Awofeso, who wrote the fiery column *Ink in my Blood*. I was captivated by the columnists' mastery of the English language. Most times I had to consult my dictionary as I read their articles. It was not until 1983 that I had my first news story published. I was a mass communication student at the University of Lagos and interning at the now-defunct national daily newspaper *National Concord*. Imagine being a journalism intern without any practical experience except for classroom exercises, and being asked to cover an earth tremor incident in a nearby state! That was the challenge I was presented with by the news editor in the absence of any staff reporter to cover this major assignment.

Shortly before I was due to leave for the assignment, which would have been a difficult one for me, a senior reporter showed up, and I had to accompany him instead. It was a learning experience for me to see how the incident was covered, but I was sad when my by-line was not included in the story, which was the lead in the newspaper the next day.

For the next three weeks or so, I was taught how to write news stories from press statements and reports that were edited but not published. I felt frustrated and was not sure if I wanted to continue the internship. However, when I opened the paper the following week, to my surprise, I saw three of my stories published with my by-line. I was so excited that I showed every other intern my published stories to let them know I was no longer an "intern without a by-line". I felt encouraged to write more stories to get more by-lines. And I did, including on the front and back pages of the newspaper, where only the best stories and top news of the day are published.

The day one of my stories was published as the lead of the back page of the paper, I found out about it at the vendor's stand. We usually got copies of the paper in the office. But my curiosity to find out whether my story had been published was such that I could not wait to get to the office. So as usual, I stopped by the vendor's stand in the morning to see the headline stories and possibly get a free copy to flip through. The headline of the lead story on the back page looked like that of the story I had submitted the previous day, but it seemed unlikely the story I was seeing could be the same one I had turned in. When I eventually realised the story was mine and that of a fellow intern, I was so excited that I was tempted to tell the vendor and other readers that I had written one of the major stories in the newspaper they were reading.

By the time I completed my internship, I had amassed many published news and feature stories, which made me a star among my colleagues when I returned to school. Only a few of us could boast of published stories in national newspapers.

After my internship, I continued writing, not only for *National Concord*, but for any newspapers that were willing to publish my stories and opinion articles. I was always on the lookout for newspapers to write for, especially among the new ones that needed content to fill their pages, and I regularly sent them my articles by post. I even sent an opinion piece to *The Guardian* newspaper in their first year of publication, even though I doubted that they would publish me since they had an array of top writers and contributors. The piece was published with minimal editing, a major encouragement to me to keep writing for the newspapers without any pay. I was just interested in getting published, and I succeeded beyond my expectations.

The link between being a journalist and a Christian didn't occur to me until about 1997, when I founded a Christian media group known as Journalists for Christ.

Journalist for Christ

Even though I was working for a secular newspaper, *The Punch*, the need to live up to the Christian faith I profess in my writings dawned on me more than ever before. I became conscious of wanting to fulfil God's purpose for my life in journalism.

In addition to ethics of the media profession, which spell out guidelines for a high standard of practice, biblical injunctions about being truthful and not bearing false witness strengthened my resolve to be an ambassador for Christ in the newsroom. I became more interested in being the "voice of the voiceless" and highlighting the plight of the poor in my reports.

Beyond writing for newspapers, I have over the years been consciously writing on journalism issues from a Christian perspective in newsletters, tracts, and books. In my missionary journalist role, I have been inspired to promote faith-based journalism practice through books like *Wisdom for Journalists, Excelling in Journalism, Purpose-Driven Journalism*, and *Reporter Extraordinaire*, which I authored.

These books were mainly inspired by presentations, discussions, and testimonies at Christian journalism fellowships in Nigeria and abroad. After listening to the testimony of Declan Okpalaeke, Nigeria's first overall winner of the CNN/MultiChoice African Journalist of the Year, I had to transcribe the audio recording and interview him on some of the insights he shared. As a result, I came up with the book *Reporter Extraordinaire*, from which many young Christian and non-Christian journalists have said they learnt a lot of lessons.

I remember being woken up one Sunday afternoon by a young journalist who said she had just finished reading *Purpose-Driven Journalism*. Before reading the book, she told me, she had been trying hard to reconcile her Christian convictions with her day-to-day experiences in the profession.

"I am glad to have read your book, which has answered many of the questions I have always wanted answers to on how to be a committed Christian and a journalist," she concluded, then requested to become a member of our fellowship.

The weekly opinion columns I have written in the now defunct *New Age* newspaper and at *The Nation*, where I worked until recently, have always been informed by the principle of "What would Jesus write?". Much as I like to write, I do not believe in writing for writing's sake. When I was the editor of *The Nation on*

Sunday and had the opportunity to write a column, it took me a while to decide to write one, despite pressure from a close friend who encouraged me that this would enhance my status. When I finally decided to write the column, I chose not to comment only on national issues. I would sometimes write about personal issues, experiences, and advice, which some readers thought were mundane, but many others enjoyed reading and could relate with. Twice, when I wrote about my wife on Valentine's Day, I got more responses to those pieces than to other articles on "serious" issues. Finding a topic to write on every week could sometimes be tough. There were weeks I struggled to find a topic and opted to give up my columns to guest writers.

One writing habit I sometimes find difficult to control is waiting till the last minute to write. I'm not too good at writing in bits, so, however close the deadline is, if I'm not in the mood to write, I find it difficult to write. Some of my best writing has, incidentally, been done under pressure to meet a deadline. Yet even when I'm not writing on paper or computer, I'm writing in my head. Lead paragraphs come to my mind, and I voice them out loud to know if they are good enough. There are days when my wife has served me dinner and is waiting for me to start eating, but I am lost in thought, thinking of a headline or paragraphs and saying things she can't comprehend. When I find it difficult to resist the ideas coming to my mind, I usually take the time to write them down.

Praying about what to write and about my journalism work was not something I used to do deliberately until I read a lecture by a former *New York Times* writer, John McCandlish Philips, entitled "Faith in the Daily News Chase", in which he spoke about how he excelled through prayer. Philips stated, "I prayed silently on my way to nearly all assignments, asking the Lord to help me, to guide me, to get me below the surface, to give me all the content I needed for a first-rate report."

In my work as a media career development specialist, writing on social media, Facebook particularly, has helped me to reach my target audience. Three years ago, I decided to write almost every day on one media career issue or another with the aim of compiling the series into a book. I couldn't write on some days, and other days I had to respond to the questions and feedback from a previous publication. *The Journalist You Ought to Be*, which I published in 2016, is a compilation of my Facebook and notebook writings. I'm not sure I would have had time to write the complete book if I hadn't opted for the social media option. For my postings and media career articles for journalists, I didn't have to try too hard to find what to write about. There was always one thing or another to write about from my daily work, meetings and programmes I participated in, or a media-related posting on Facebook.

I once saw a post by a journalist that suggested many of the media awards meted out within the country of Nigeria were not worth much. Another journalist supported the claim, wondering what the pedigree of those making the assessment was. My response was a write-up titled "No Award Is Too Small". A photo journalist who won the Photo Journalist of the Year Award in 2015 said it was one of the most inspiring professional articles he had read in his thirty years of practicing.

I read a compilation of short profiles I had written to some journalists participating in a media fellowship and noticed how we didn't sufficiently articulate our accomplishments. So I came up with an article called "What You Are Not Saying about Yourself".

I regard being able to write on various platforms as a privilege I take seriously. I therefore do my best not to abuse the privilege, being careful about what I write and how I write. I'm aware that not everybody can write professionally, and some who can don't have the opportunity to get published. I feel personally fulfilled about my writing when I'm able to connect with the inner feelings of my readers, when they write back to say that I spoke their mind or inspired them.

We live in a world and time where daily living and survival is a challenge for many. Offering advice in my writings gives me the satisfaction of helping readers who have lost hope and are not sure what to do in the depressing circumstance they have found themselves. When some journalists were sacked from *The Guardian* newspaper in Nigeria in 2016, my advice for them and other journalists in the column, "No Tears for Sacked Journalists," was that they shouldn't cry over spilled milk. Considering the economic recession and new digital options, which have left media houses with no alternative but to retrench staff, my counsel in the piece was that the affected journalists and any other person who has lost his or her job should consider other options for survival. They could, for instance, offer editorial services, blog, set up their own website, or develop content for websites. I received feedback from a recently retired medical doctor for whom my suggestions were invaluable and helpful.

Just like other writers, I have had my own share of agonies and unfulfilled writing dreams, but I have learnt not to be discouraged. One scripture that has kept me going is 1 Samuel 30:6:

> *Now David was greatly distressed, for the people spoke of stoning him, because the soul of all the people was grieved, every man for his sons and his daughters. But David strengthened himself in the Lord his God (NKJV).*

My first major attempt at publishing a book was in 1998 after a three-month advanced journalism training at Thomson Foundation, Wales, United Kingdom. It was to be an account of how I applied and was accepted for the fellowship against all odds. God had granted me favour to get the media fellowship and to experience my first travel outside my country. The manuscript was completed and typed, but never got published. Another writing project with which I was unsuccessful was "God in the News," which involved highlighting references to God in media reports. After a few months of publishing the series on a weekly basis, I can't explain why I was unable to continue writing it.

At a couples' event I attended with my wife Ronke, she was asked what I enjoyed doing most. She gave exactly the same answer I had written down in response to the question: writing. Beyond being a professional journalist, writing, as far as I'm concerned, is God's gift to express my feelings about issues and situations in which I find myself. Writing is definitely not as lucrative as many other professions, but I thank God for the gift of being a journalist and writer.

Lillian Tindyebwa

Uganda

Lillian Tindyebwa holds an MA in Literature from Makerere University. She is a founding member of Uganda Women Writers Association, FEMRITE.

She is also the executive director of Uganda Faith Writers Association, a Christian-based writing organisation. She is a published author. Her first novel, *Recipe for Disaster*, published by Fountain Publishers, is used as a reader in secondary schools in Uganda.

Her other works are mainly short stories, with the most successful one titled *Looking for My Mother*. It deals with problems of rejection and teenage pregnancy.

Lillian is married to Stephen, and they have five children. She lives in Kampala, Uganda.

The Right Path

Some people's journeys have been smooth and so ostensibly ordained that they had no other choice but to follow the beaten path. I recall listening to a radio talk show in which someone was criticizing a leader for apparently grooming his son to take over from him. In defence of the leader, a member of the panel said that it was absolutely normal for a family to guide the children according to a tradition into the family career path.

"Look at the chiefs of old," he said.

Mmm, I thought. *Perfect fit—like a pea in a pod.*

I, on the other hand, seem to have been dragged kicking and screaming to the writing table. I see now that a lot of events in my life were the rugged steps that led me to the point where I hesitantly picked up a pen and sat down, trying hard to focus my eyes on the label on my desk that reads: "Your search ends here; you are a Christian writer."

The turning point was 1959, when my older sister and I were both still preschoolers. That was the year when the wispy layers started to fall off my eyes, and I began to awaken slowly as though coming from a deep sleep. As the layers came off, more of the world around me emerged from its shell, and I began to appreciate things hitherto hidden from me.

Everywhere I turned, the world seemed to vie for the attention of my two little eyes: bees, flowers, birds, caterpillars that I feared like death, and cranes that laid their eggs in the swamp at the bottom of our homestead. One day my cousin and I came across a crane's nest. My cousin had the bright idea of taking an egg from the nest. Immediately the mother crane came after him, taking long strides, its wings spread wide although it wouldn't fly. It was a spectacle to behold!

My cousin too had long legs, and he ran determinedly as we both screamed and shouted. When the mother crane had almost caught up with him, he had an even brighter idea. Gently placing the egg on the ground, he fled for his life. The mother crane stopped in her tracks, picked up the egg with her beak, and slowly carried it back to the comfort of the swamp.

At other times when we were not in the mood to antagonise the cranes, we would sing, and the cranes would dance. I still remember the song: *Tuuha, sandararano!* (Crane, crane, dance!). We would repeat it several times, and the cranes would spread out their wings and jump around in an unnamed dance.

One evening as my older sister and I were playing in the compound outside my parents' little mud-and-wattle house, we saw our father on his bicycle as he turned the corner onto the hill road that led home. It was the end of the day, and he was coming back from his job as an English teacher at a local school. He had a cardboard box on the carrier of the bicycle. It was unusual for him to come home with such a bountiful-looking box because life back then was lived on a shoestring. We stopped our play and waited with bated breath. What was he carrying? Bread? *Mandazi* (a fried bread treat like a doughnut)? Guavas? What could be the contents of the box? For little girls from a rural setting, our imagination could not stretch any further.

We greeted him as he untied the box from the bicycle. He carried it in his hands, and we followed him inside the house. He too seemed anxious to open it. My mum had laid out tea for him, but he was too excited to eat. Another man arrived soon after him, and together they opened the box and carefully got the contents out. It was a rectangular thing.

"What is that, Father?" I asked.

"A radio," he answered.

"A what?"

"Radio. It speaks."

"It speaks?!" I said, incredulous.

"Yes, it will give us news, and we shall get to know what happens elsewhere in the country and the world," he said.

We simply stared and waited eagerly for the miracle box to start speaking and connecting us to the world. Once it came on, we all burst into a little celebration song.

The Right Path

That was how we received the radio. It was a brown rectangular box. Its power came from a battery that looked like a perfect brick except for its blue colour.

At first the radio was placed on the dining table, but eventually my father and his friend and my mother agreed that they had to get a tall table specially made so that only the grown-ups would be able to operate it. Not that any of us would have been daring enough to try, but my parents had to ensure that any chance of temptation for us children was eliminated. In two days the table arrived, and the radio took its place in our living room.

From then on, the box and the brick sat connected side by side on the high stool as if in a silent friendship. There it was, the radio, making its way into places never reached before. Ours was not the only home in our neighbourhood with the box, but it was definitely one of the first. It was to become one of the major things that pervaded the atmosphere of our home for years to come, making its indelible mark.

Although my father was a teacher of English, getting used to the news reader's voice was challenging for him. I remember him in the evening ritual of listening to the news. He would ensure that there was total silence in the room, and then he would listen as though his life depended on it. If he could not get us to remain silent, he would stand up and place his ear next to the radio, hoping to catch whatever he could.

One evening there was a little drama at our house. As my father listened with his ear to the radio, a woman who was our neighbour and a habitual drunkard was on her way home. As per usual, she entered our house. Many of our neighbours would do that, especially if they could hear that the radio was on. When the lady saw what my father was doing, she came and stood next to him in an attempt to imitate him. She tilted her head as if she too was trying to hear what was being broadcast. My father simply ignored her, acting like he was too absorbed in his ritual. It was hilarious for us children, but we did not laugh out loud. We just covered our mouths with our little hands and laughed. We always enjoyed the antics of the village drunkards.

On its high pedestal in the corner of our living room, the radio remained as a symbol of things emerging from hidden places and stretching into the future.

It stood like a mighty grandfather clock, and it brought the rest of the world into our house: news, announcements of deaths and funerals, music and songs, greetings and fun.

The purpose of this radio was to gain general knowledge and to familiarize ourselves with the English language, which was to become a medium of instruction. The local languages were still very much in use, but so was English. No wonder by mid-primary I was already topping my class in this language.

The most remarkable thing about this time was that it was a period of transition. New ways of life and other foreign influences were coming, while others were going. It was as if new things were on trial to see if they would bring the promises they had made all of us believe and expect. Mine was a second generation of recipients of an external school system brought to us in another tongue. It was a time of great expectations, of hopes built on many things not yet proved by time.

Years earlier a fire had been started, a fire of revival. Christianity had come to my country. Chiefs and their families had welcomed the co-labourers with Christ, reluctantly at first and then wholeheartedly. Playing the role of the colt to Christianity was education. Yes, there had to be a good dose of education, otherwise how would one read the Word of God? Therefore, from the courts of the chiefs and kings, the fire of reading and writing spread and started the transformation that saw new ways increasingly replacing old ones.

In the 1930s and 1940s, the revival fire lit in Gahini, Rwanda, reached our village in Uganda amid the dense woodlands inhabited by cattle keepers living on milk and plantains. The rolling hills around the homesteads suddenly filled with the sound of people singing new songs of freedom. They had been set free from years of idolatry and hopelessness. Voices of hope were carried by the gentle breeze of the countryside, crossing hills and valleys, reaching people. This fire proved to be unstoppable.

Soon the village paths were filled with a different sound—that of trampling feet. Some feet were running to get to school on time, most were bare, but now there was the bright hope of wearing shoes one day. Some of these feet would one day cross oceans on their way to far-off lands. The eyes of the older generations saw their children dressed in smart uniforms and going to schools, something that

The Right Path

was previously unheard of. They saw a new world opening up before them, and they lived through their children, placing all their hopes for the future into their new-found ways of life.

My father had lost his father, and as he sat with his mother in their little hut, they heard of new things, of the truth that there was a living God. They heard of it through the lips of preachers who spoke the good news of a Saviour called Jesus.

For a house that no longer had anybody to call a father, the idea of a Father in heaven spoke volumes, and they embraced the message unreservedly. They gave their lives to Jesus once for all. In a village nearby lived a young lady who was to become my mother. She too heard this message and received it. The old was going, and the new was coming in. When they were finally joined together in holy matrimony, my parents set up a home that was built on Christ Jesus.

One day in the early 1960s, my father came home and called my mother aside.

"I am going to build a school. Not a primary but a secondary school," he said.

In those days, secondary schools in the country could be counted on the fingers of one hand. Who was this young man to pull off such a venture? It sounded bigger than life, but he was serious.

My mother was apprehensive and asked many questions. When she was convinced, she gave all the support that she could. Soon the buildings were up, and inspectors came all the way from the capital to visit the site. Permission was granted, and the secondary school was soon full of students.

That was not just an achievement for my father but also another stepping stone for me. It meant that I was fortunate enough at that time, when many people couldn't even read, to live in a home that had a library. It was modest, but it gave me access to books. I remember after my primary level during the long vacation before joining secondary school I was literally a bookworm, buried in this little room. I discovered famous American classics such as *Tom Sawyer* and *Huckleberry Finn* and British writers such as Shakespeare and Dickens. There were also many non-fiction books on science, geography, and English. I was learning at my own pace and interest, and that worked best for me.

Besides the library books, my father also had his personal books, especially Christian ones. I think it was during that same holiday that I came across his old copy of *Pilgrim's Progress*. The cover was torn, and I was only able to tell that it was his due to the notes he had made in the margins. I read and finished it and benefitted from the notes as well. He also had Billy Graham's *World Aflame* and many more. My father also bought magazines such as *Time* and *Newsweek* as well as an East African magazine called *Drum*. This helped to cultivate in me the love of books and reading, which has been so pivotal for me as a writer.

Later when I was on another vacation after my "O" level examinations, I had a dream. Unfortunately, I cannot remember the details of this dream, but I thought at the time that it was telling me I should be a writer. I even got a notebook and started to write something, but I didn't continue. However, the idea did not die. It kept popping into my head, and I always believed that time would come when I would bring it to pass.

Looking back now, I think I did not continue to try my hand at writing partly due to a lack of self-belief. The lack of role models was a big problem. Now I see that although I read a lot, these were books far removed from my experience. It took a long time for me to get to the point where I believed that I could do what their authors did. That is my theory anyway, but it could have some good truth.

One day around 1991 as I sat at Alliance Française in Kampala, where I had gone to polish up my French, the idea popped up again. I would go a little early and sit and wait for the classes to start. They had a library with lots of books and magazines. As I waited for my class to start, the idea of writing came back to me. This time around, I responded with determination to accomplish the project I had left pending for such a long time.

My first book simply flowed out of the tip of my pen as if it had been anxiously waiting to be set free. The book, *Recipe for Disaster*, was finally published in 1994. It is for young adults, and it deals with problems of peer pressure in the wake of the HIV/AIDS pandemic. This book was followed by a short story titled *Looking for My Mother*. The story deals with the problems of teenage pregnancy and how to act with a sense of responsibility when faced with a traumatic experience. Other stories followed.

The Right Path

Although this novel and several short stories were published, I did not make the decision to specifically write Christian books until 2009 when I and some friends decided to form Uganda Faith Writers Association. We saw it as a platform for Christian writers, and I do believe that through it young and upcoming writers will have a chance to find role models that inspire them to write stories that are their own, so as to bring glory to the Lord.

We all know the saying that goes something like this: "Until the lions have their own historians, the history of the hunt will always favour the hunter." Likewise, until Christians write their own stories or sing their own music, history will always favour the others.

My journey as a writer is far from being over. I feel wisps are still peeling off my eyes. I have come to believe that this never ends and that we keep discovering new things that bring hope and renewal. I now see a new countryside speeding by as I traverse this territory, and I laugh as I pick the flowers, the fruits and, yes, also stop to breathe in the cool breeze, knowing that at last I am on the right path.

Pusonnam Yiri

Nigeria

Pusonnam Yiri is an author, speaker, and trainer. He is the president of Taskworkers Ventures and chairman/managing director of Nachau Turomale Centre LTD. He obtained a diploma in mass communication from the University of Jos; a Bachelor of Arts in theology (missions and evangelism) from ECWA Theological Seminary, Jos, and a Master of Theology (systematic theology) from Theological College of Northern Nigeria. He is the author of *151 Short Stories*, *The Meaningful Life*, and the Reconciliation series, which includes *Slavery of the Mind*, *Blindness of the Mind*, *Storms of the Mind*, and *Injuries of the Mind*.

Pusonnam conducts seminars on book writing and living a meaningful life. He is married to Helen and blessed with three children: Pwasollam, Pusam, and Pamale.

No One Is Useless: A Story of God's Grace

Imagine a leaf dropping from a tree's branch with no hope of surviving, then suddenly getting another chance to be reattached to the tree and live even better than before. For me, becoming a writer is like being that leaf, granted a unique chance to develop only by the grace of God.

"No one is useless" is a major theme in my writing journey, a theme quite closely connected with the story of my life. At an early stage I was a slow learner. Some people in our house called me by strange names that described it. A lady who lived with us made her own description of me worse by making fun of me in a way that portrayed me as a dull person.

I gave my life to Jesus Christ towards the end of secondary school. It was a decision that dramatically changed my life and journey, leading to an improved awareness of myself, a perception that eventually worked well for me as a writer.

The conscious process of discovering my writing potential began at the University of Jos in Plateau State, Nigeria, where I did a diploma programme in mass communication. My speech communication course lecturer commended my speech writing and presentation, and the feedback from my classmates confirmed the commendation. Among other skills, I learnt news writing, drama, and feature writing, which were fundamental to my writing ministry.

After I had written a few scripts for drama presentations, I wrote the film script *Good for Evil*, which I later converted to a novel. It is the story of maltreatment of an orphan and forgiveness. I wrote another film script titled *Born Bad*. Both films were produced and released.

Moreover, I developed a strong interest in proverb development, which became a vital tool in shaping my ability to discover, analyse, and develop ideas. Proverb development involves critical thinking. I would observe nature, human behaviour, and events to create life-changing proverbs. I formed the discipline of documenting the sayings as I created them, as well as the dates, places, and sometimes the time and occasion of each development. To date, I have developed more than two thousand such proverbs, which I often use in speaking and writing. I have enjoyed using the sayings, especially in my novels, to enrich the dialogue of some of my characters. A few of my favourites are: *A dry leaf under a tree is a strong warning to the green ones* (21-11-99); *The future may not be for us, but it can be better because of us* (16-6-2004).

My seminary experiences have also exposed me to understanding writing, especially the need for wide reading and proper acknowledgement of research sources.

My central writing topics are purpose and the development of potential. Reading Myles Munroe, author of *Releasing Your Potential* and *Maximizing Your Potential*, was helpful in my choice of central topics.

Writing with a Purpose

I used stories in speaking at the first seminary I attended. A few students who were ministers encouraged me to compile the stories into a book for them to use. They had seen in me what I could not effectively see in myself. The challenge encouraged me, and I wrote my first book, published in 2007. I write to help people understand the purpose of life and how to achieve it for reconciliation to God. My second book was written as a result of a radio programme I participated in. Many of the text messages and calls we received during and after the programme pointed towards two important questions: what to do and how to do it. After the programme and other similar interactions on potential, I felt convinced to write a book that would respond to the two questions.

In 2010, I released *Slavery of the Mind: Discover What You Can Do and How to Do It*. This became a ground-breaking book for me as a writer. Many people were encouraged by the book. The feedback encouraged me to start the Reconciliation Series. *Blindness of the Mind: No One Is Useless* is the second book in the series. It also became successful, and I continued to write other books.

I also write because I want to ensure that the right values are captured and saved for generations to come to prevent the influence of false teaching. Finally, I write because I want to be an example to other potential writers who might gain the courage to start writing as a result of my own progress.

Encouragement to Keep Going

Towards the end of my mass communication training, a friend and classmate told me that he would become a musician and I would become a writer. His prediction has since been fulfilled for both of us. Having a family that is supportive has also put me in the right state of mind to write and to grow as a writer. I am of the view that a person who fails in his family responsibility will hardly be effective in ministry.

I have received encouragement as a writer from several sources right from the beginning. One source of encouragement was a former lecturer who saw the manuscript of my first book, *151 Life Changing Short Stories and Their Lessons*, and paid for some copies in advance. The money was useful in my effort to produce the book. After the printing, I gave him copies worth the value of his money.

After the book release, the feedback I received from readers was a great source of encouragement. I had the courage to continue because the readers had accepted me as a writer. I would probably have been discouraged if the readers had rejected me.

I felt encouraged too when the first seminary I attended accepted my request for my first published book to be presented at a programme organised in the school. My editors, both within and outside Nigeria, have also done a great job of encouraging me. Their input has made a big difference in my writings.

A book has to be screened to ascertain its worthiness before it is accepted for sale by any standard bookstores. The acceptance of my first book by Africa Christian Textbooks (ACTS) for sale in its bookstores was encouraging. ACTS later gave me the opportunity to participate in a writers and editors workshop, which they organised in association with Langham Partnership International (LPI) in 2010. It was there that I learnt some important and life-changing book writing ideas that enhanced my writing journey. I developed greater confidence and motivation to write effectively and to train others in writing as a result of that contact.

The decision by ACTS to publish my Reconciliation Series books was a big breakthrough. Based on what I was told, I was the first fiction writer to be published on its platform. This gave the books broad-based distribution and enlarged the audience network. Other fiction writers might have the opportunity of getting published as a result of the open door.

I also felt motivated when I was informed that a professor in a secular university used one of my books, *Blindness of the Mind*, in training his students. I was happy when I saw the question paper with my name among a few giants and famous writers in literature. The greatest part of the story was when the professor told me that two of his students gave their lives to Jesus as a result of his teaching the text. The archbishop of my church denomination was also very encouraging. He bought many copies of my books in the Reconciliation Series to give out to people.

Encouragement also came from Media Associates International when I was invited in 2013 to attend its *Training Trainers* workshop in Nairobi, Kenya. After the training, I was given a few opportunities on the platform to share my thoughts as a writer and trainer in writing. I have expanded my network of friends who are also writers and trainers as a result of my relationship with MAI.

Overcoming Obstacles

In the northern part of Nigeria where I live, many people have faced emotional trauma from the activities of insurgents and fanatics. Many people have lost their loved ones and possessions in crises. My wife was also directly affected. She lost her cousin and his two boys. I too have had my share of loss in the crises. Some church buildings were burnt and many Christians persecuted. Almost on a daily basis, we wake up with news of death, destruction, and security breaches. Only by the grace of God is it possible to concentrate and write in such a difficult situation.

Furthermore, we have had problems with inadequate power supply. Imagine a situation where you often have to wait for power supply for hours to charge your laptop. In urgent situations, the option is to either use a generator or go to a place where power is more stable. This is frustrating, especially when ideas are pressing for release.

It was challenging growing an organisation, providing for my family, and writing at the same time, especially without a salary. Balancing the three has not been easy, yet I have been able by the grace of God to grow in writing.

The task of releasing my first book was challenging. I did not have a computer, nor did I know how to type well. The first draft was handwritten. After that I took it to a business centre for typing, then to some people who helped edit it. I had neither a mainline publisher nor the money to print. I made a special arrangement with a printer who was kind enough to print for me on special terms. His contribution was indeed memorable in my writing journey.

A friend of mine later gave me a desktop computer—my first computer. It may not be as valuable to me now as it was then, but it was a great gift. Eventually I bought a laptop, which was vital in speeding up my work. My computer skills have developed. I no longer use the handwritten approach to write my books but type them myself on my laptop. This has simplified my writing process.

My Writing Journey: Anchored in Faith

A proverb asks, "When a fish marries a bird, where will they live after the wedding?" This indeed is a difficult union, full of confusion. Similarly, without my Christian faith my writing journey would have been full of confusion and many difficulties. Jesus is everything I have. Without him I cannot do anything. Even my academic qualifications are theological. That means my effectiveness in writing and lifestyle are anchored by my faith in God. This has given me my central theme in writing and methods of communicating it effectively.

It was after giving my life to Jesus that I also realised more fully my potential. That is why the subtitle of this story focuses on God's grace. My faith also gave me compassion, the ability to forgive, and the strength to endure in difficult circumstances.

My desire for excellence is enhanced by my faith. I see excellence as an act of worship because God deserves the best.

My motive for writing is also shaped by my faith in God. I see my writings as tools for helping people know God better and grow effectively in their use of gifts. Fiction is the genre I find most appealing. It gives me the opportunity to create and push the boundaries of human discoveries in God's master plan. It also helps me to explore and bring into reality things that are unimaginable to unstretched minds.

A Foundation Laid on the Rock

Perseverance in difficult times is not possible without first discovering a worthy task. My vision is "knowledge-empowered people using their gifts and writing their values for reconciliation to God". This to me is a worthy task for the glory of God.

The story Jesus shared of two builders reflects my secret for surviving difficult times:

> They are like a man building a house, who dug down deep and laid the foundation on rock. When a flood came, the torrent struck that house but could not shake it, because it was well built. But the one who hears my words and does not put them into practice is like a man who built a house on the ground without a foundation. The moment the torrent struck that house, it collapsed and its destruction was complete (Luke 6:48-49, NIV).

I desire to always build on the Rock. Even though the journey is not always easy, my faith in God's ability to finish his projects keeps me going.

I see my writings as medical drugs (ideas) that need to be provided continually to cure many diseases (problems). Many people would be affected negatively if I didn't write. My goal of reaching people with solutions to problems helps me build my muscles to keep writing in spite of challenges.

My conviction that writing is the most effective tool for capturing and communicating godly values in this generation and subsequent ones is also helpful in discouraging times. I think of our children, who need to have access to godly values. It is our responsibility to preserve these values. I worry about our elders who have died with their values uncommunicated. There is nothing much we can now do to gain knowledge of those values. I honestly don't want that to happen in my generation.

Offences can also cause huge setbacks in writing. My desire for forgiveness and reconciliation helps sustain me. Nobody can live well in isolation. We must learn to co-exist with others, and in this process, offences must come. I am learning to set my forgiveness on automatic, functioning even before an offence. In that way

I will, by God's grace, enhance my creative moments even in the midst of offences. It is not easy, but it is possible with God.

My Greatest Satisfaction

> Sir, God bless you. I was in a confused state of mind, not knowing what life has in store for me until this morning when I came in contact with your book, *Slavery of the Mind*. After going through it, my life experienced a massive transformation. Truly, I have never been challenged like now. I would like to hear more from you, because you are my mentor, encourager and my new friend in CHRIST JESUS.

This is feedback I received from a reader. Such is my greatest satisfaction. It confirms the achievement of my goal, which is helping people discover and achieve the purpose of life—reconciliation to God. Unlike verbal communication, which lasts for just a moment, my books will outlive me. This means the testimonies of transformation will be discussed for many years to come, God willing.

Fulfilling the Master Plan

A messenger communicates the message of his sender. Since I am empowered by God to write, he is the one who inspires the ideas for my books and motivates me to write. Ideas are hidden in our societies: in the streets, markets, hospitals, offices, schools, and in difficult and happy moments. Only those who seek will find them. A writer who is able to clearly identify a problem to solve is likely to encounter relevant ideas that provide solutions.

Once, my older sister and I visited one of our parents' neighbours. When my sister saw a big rooster there, she commended the patience of the owner for allowing it to grow to that level of maturity instead of slaughtering it for meat. Similarly, what I am doing is only because of the grace of my Owner. I need to write always as my way of thanking him for the chance to live and grow in my writing ministry. The fact that no one is useless in God's master plan is a motivation that will continue to sustain my writing and also encourage others to realise and achieve their potential for God's glory.

Solomon Andria

Côte d'Ivoire

Solomon Andria Tsimialomananarivo, PhD, was born in 1950 in Madagascar. He is married with six grown children.

He is a former lecturer at Faculte de Theologie Evangelique de l'Alliance Chretienne (West Africa Alliance Evangelical Seminary) Abidjan, Côte d'Ivoire.

Solomon is the coordinator of Langham Partnership for Literature in Francophone Africa.

He is the author of several books, including *Eglise et Mission à l'époque contemporaine* (2007), *Romans* (2012), and *Initiatives Théologiques en Afrique*.

The Writing Dream

The love of language! Language is a gift from God that enables us to communicate, exchange ideas, express our deepest feelings, and explore the universe. Because of language, we are in dialogue with God. So we might as well love it, improve it, and teach it to others. To a new generation. And the best way to teach it to others is to write.

Ever since I was young, I have always cherished the dream of leaving a heritage to posterity. A bold ambition, but I am convinced that leaving some legacy, especially an intellectual legacy, no matter how small or insignificant, will give deep moral satisfaction. Just as I have drawn great benefit from my spiritual fathers, now it is my turn to make sure that my "children" benefit from my gains.

With this goal in mind, I began to write at the age of thirty-four, and I have not stopped since, though I must confess that many of my manuscripts are still in my cupboard.

Two Men

Two men have influenced my writing. The first is John Stott, who was a leader of the worldwide evangelical movement. I was particularly impressed by two of Stott's books: the French version of *Basic Christianity*, which I read when I was twenty-one or twenty-two years old, and *I Believe in Preaching*, a book that emphasises the importance of preaching. Through his writing, Stott made known to me his three priorities in ministry: writing, preaching, and teaching. He himself wrote for millions of readers, preached to thousands, and invested in individuals, as Monty Barker says in the book *Mission as Transformation: Learning from Catalysts*.

What a joy it is to read John Stott! Here is a man of great learning who writes in simple language and in a way that is always relevant. He knows how to create a personal relationship with his readers.

Henri Blocher, the other man who has influenced my writing, is Stott's opposite in more ways than one. He is a scholar whose language is highly academic. He addresses a readership that is not as broad, as if more selective of his public. This style enables him to be quite precise in the presentation of ideas and concepts, pushing his readers to pursue their reflections as far as possible. It takes a sustained, deliberate effort to follow his thinking, but once I understand his text, his ideas stay with me for decades. I was particularly impressed with his book *In the Beginning*, which I read in French (*Revelation des Origines*). It explains the first three pages of the Bible, which deal with creation.

Writing in Big, Bold Characters

I write in French and from time to time in Malagasy and English. Most of my writings are teachings in various forms. I delight in communicating the truths of Scripture. They are universal and eternal, remaining constant in an ever-changing world. I recognize that reading does not appeal to many of the present generation. They exist in a world of images and sound and are thus drawn to the path requiring the least effort. They would rather "dialogue" with their tablets, fascinated by what they discover there. But what they discover does not necessarily edify.

Thus, at least once I gave up and dropped my writing to focus on other things. What use is it to spend months or even years writing a book that no one will read? To consult dozens of references, visit libraries, spend sleepless nights in order to produce ideas that will promote the spiritual development of believers—all that is quite a challenge. But despite the lack of interest in reading by too many of the present generation, I shall continue to write—this time in big, bold characters. Although few today may be reading, I will go on writing. I will transmit to others, especially to the young, whatever modest knowledge I possess. Perhaps my books are not read today. But tomorrow or the next day or even twenty years from now, someone will read them.

Writing for those of the present and future generations is fascinating, motivating, and challenging. I like to help readers enter into a dialogue with themselves and with other writers, to develop a culture of reflection, and to draw conclusions for themselves. As I see it, to write is to motivate readers to take responsibility for themselves in this world where one can obtain anything, at least virtually, at the touch of a button. Thinking, if it is to be enriching, necessarily involves reading. A generation that does not think is a dying generation intellectually and culturally. Is it possible to conceive of a people without culture?

Joy and Suffering

Writing has its joys and sorrows, as all writers know. There is the joy of writing. Of putting down in writing the things one has on one's heart or in one's head. The joy of choosing words and grammatical constructions. In short, the joy of freely expressing one's ideas. But the greatest joy is hearing echoes of one's book being accurately cited by another author or by a student writing a thesis or dissertation—provided that the quote is taken in context and faithfully reflects the author's thinking!

My joy was indescribable (but very discreet) when one of my readers told me he had read my book and had appreciated the message of an anecdote in that book. To illustrate a biblical point, I had told the story of a man who attended church one Sunday and the next day went to present his heartfelt thanks to the pastor. The sermon had helped him a great deal. The pastor asked him, "How did the sermon help you, then?" The man replied without hesitation, "When you said, 'Thou shalt not commit adultery,' I remembered where I had left my hat!"

It was not the anecdote itself that my reader had particularly enjoyed, but rather the message it conveyed. He had indeed grasped the thought expressed in my book. Writing is gratifying, then, not so much for the remuneration, but rather the appreciation.

The sorrows are perhaps more numerous and more intense than the joys. Discussions with editors are sometimes difficult. The author wants his message conveyed as faithfully as possible and in his own style, whereas the editor wants to sell books; his motives are sometimes commercial. He may want the author to delete a portion of the text that highlights a troubling truth that will make his customers uncomfortable. Sometimes the author will make concessions against his convictions.

On another level, waiting for the book release can be painful, even agonizing. The author waits for months, even years, for the book to come out. But the greatest pain is discovering errors, large and small, in the published book, even though the manuscript was read, re-read, revised, and corrected.

I remember one painful experience, so painful that I am not likely ever to forget it. I had prepared an explanatory and summary diagram for one of my books, a diagram that I believed to be clear. However, when the book was released, a single error made the diagram say the exact opposite of what I meant! It stated the very opposite of my theological position on a delicate topic. I would have liked for every copy in circulation to be destroyed immediately so that a revised and corrected version could be printed. But it was an experience, not a failure. Perfection is not to be found in this world, but the author must strive for perfection.

Writing: a Way to Intellectual Enrichment

English and French are languages that I learnt at school, in contrast to my mother tongue, the language that, in the words of Isaac Zokoué, "leaps of its own accord from soul to lips. In that tongue, words and thoughts have no need of seeking one another out." When I write in one of these European languages, I draw near to a form of expression that is accurate and precise. I strive for perfection. On the other hand, when I am writing in my own language, I am already in that which is accurate and precise. I enjoy the dialectic between European languages and my mother tongue, between theoretical knowledge and daily living, between grand ideas and concrete realities. In other words, I communicate grand ideas in learnt language, and I often share my deep personal feelings in the form of poetry in my mother tongue.

Writing shapes language and forges thinking. Writing also shapes one's neighbour, helping him or her to discover the same treasures as oneself and to revel in new ideas. To write is to share with others the graces and blessings of God.

The Impact of Experience

I learnt from one of my brothers that my mother, who was eighty-five years old at the time, had only a few days to live. Her strength was failing rapidly. My reflex was to write her a poem, which I hoped I would have the opportunity to read to her before she closed her eyes for eternity.

I recalled a specific event that had taken place forty years before when I had told my mother of my decision to serve God in full-time ministry. At the time, I was working as an engineer for a big private company in Antananarivo, Madagascar. After just one year, I had decided to resign from that job and became the first fulltime student worker of the Malagasy IFES-related movement. My mother accepted my decision, but with fear. According to my culture, I had to keep on supporting my father and my mother financially.

The Writing Dream

I wrote the poem in my mother tongue. It began like this:

> *Nekenao tokoa, ry Neny,*
> *Ny nialako tamin'ny asako,*
> *Ho mpanompo, hitoriteny*
> *Amin'ireo sakaiza namako.*
> *[Mom, you really accepted*
> *That from my job I departed.*
> *The gospel I would then preach*
> *To my friends, to them each.*

Sadly, my mother passed away before she could listen to the poem. I read the poem at her funeral, not for her, but for my children and my nephews. A journalist who was present at the funeral decided to publish it the next day in a local newspaper. How surprised I was when others of my generation identified with the speaker in the poem and sent me thank you notes. "The poem greatly comforted me," one said. I could not have imagined the impact of this poem on others since I had written it specifically for my mother.

I learnt from this that some readers identify with the characters we present or create in our books and appropriate our message for themselves. What a great moral satisfaction!

From One Dream to Another

When my first book was published twenty-five years ago, it was a great joy mixed with fear. I really fear the reactions of potential readers. I have to wait for some years before I receive positive reactions, as they need time to assess the content of the book.

The dream that I cherished as a young man came true after some decades, since I was able to write and publish a number of books.

But my second and final dream is yet to be realized: the dream of seeing the current generation and future generations develop a culture of reading. What joy will be mine when not only John Stott and Henri Blocher, but also Kwame Bediako and Tokunboh Adeyemo, Tite Tiénou, and Yusufu Turaki will be read!

Then African Christianity will be a thinking and motivating faith. Then I will see confirmed the words of Kwame Bediako: "The center of gravity of Christianity has moved to Africa."

Stella Chika Okoronkwo

Côte d'Ivoire

Stella is a self-motivated, trilingual professional with two master's degrees in communication and development. She has worked as programme and communication manager in international organisations and as a lecturer in various universities.

She was a member of faculty in past LittWorld training conferences.

Stella has interacted effectively and collegially with different teams and senior executives from multi-cultural settings, which has earned her respect and recognition. She has been involved with Christian, humanitarian, and development programmes. She is author of fifteen books in both French and English. She is married to Rev. Gilbert Okoronkwo. They have three young adult children and one grandchild.

How I Became A Writer

"Writing is an art," they say. For some, it is a hobby or pastime. But it can actually become your life, your calling, platform, and ministry. Three reasons come to mind when I ponder why and how I became a writer. The first is that both in secondary school and in the university, my teachers used to tell me I wrote very good essays, both in French and English, although I am not really sure I believed them. After graduation and moving to Kenya, I decided to verify what my lecturers said by submitting an article to *Parents*, a Kenyan magazine. Because I was not so sure my article was good enough to be accepted for publishing, I used a pen name—Jonathan Edwards. To my greatest surprise, my article was immediately accepted and published! Now I was mad at myself for using someone else's name. I photocopied my article, typed out my own name, and pasted it on top of the pen name so that people would see that I was the one who had written the article. I became jealous of whoever had that name. That was how my writing journey began around 1990.

In the ensuing months, I submitted articles to other magazines, and they too were published. I finally became convinced that I could write good stuff, and I plunged myself head-on into the business of writing.

The second reason I began writing was that I encountered a scarcity of Christian literature as a student of Modern Languages in Côte d'Ivoire in 1980/81, to the extent that when I needed tracts for evangelism I had to buy them with the little pocket money I had. I looked to heaven and did what Jacob did in Bethel when he was fleeing Esau to go to Laban.

> Then Jacob made a vow, saying, "If God will be with me, and keep me in this way that I am going, and give me bread to eat and clothing to put on, so that I come back to my father's house in peace, then the LORD shall be my God. And this stone which I have set as a pillar shall be God's house, and of all that You give me I will surely give a tenth to You" (Genesis 28:20-22, NASB).

My own vow was both somewhat similar and different. It was similar in the sense that I was in a foreign land just as Jacob had been, as I was born in Nigeria. It was different because my vow was about writing, not about visiting an uncle. I promised God that I would definitely write books and tracts if he helped me finish my studies and get settled. Also, I did not lay a stone as a memorial. My memorial was written boldly in my heart as a vow that I have never forgotten. The hostel where I lived, which still stands today, may also serve as a physical memorial. As one enters from the side of the French school, it is the first room of the first building of the Mermoz Campus at the Houphouet Boigny University, Cocody, Abidjan in Côte d'Ivoire.

Meeting the Needs of Readers

My first book was a Sunday school curriculum. One day around 1992, I walked into a Sunday school class at the Nairobi Pentecostal Church and sat down. The teachers looked at me curiously. The class was for ten to fifteen-year-old new converts who were being prepared for baptism. I observed as their teachers taught, and I also looked at the curriculum they were using. At the end of the class, I told the teachers that their teaching was interesting, but their curriculum was above the level of their students and was written in a different culture. I asked them if they would like me to develop a new curriculum adapted to the African culture. They jumped up and began praising God. They told me they had been praying to God that he would send someone to help them develop a new curriculum for the new converts class. I said to them, "Now your prayers have been answered, and I am here to help you."

Within a couple of weeks, I developed a sixteen-lesson curriculum for them and asked them to begin using it while I joined their class to evaluate and revise the curriculum. After the curriculum had been used for a couple of years, it was published in 1998 under the title *Growing in Christ When Young*. It contained stories and pictures that made the lessons interesting for young people. I was surprised when someone told me a group of adults was using it for their Bible study. I made another vow to the Lord that if the book did well in the market, I would write other books for his glory. The book did very well, and many more books have been written since then to the glory of God.

How I Became A Writer

The Barnabases Along My Writing Journey

Barnabas was a great encourager to Paul and Peter during their missionary journeys as recorded in the book of Acts. Similarly, God placed a few Barnabases along my writing journey too. Shortly after developing the Sunday school curriculum, I won a scholarship to attend a curriculum development workshop at Cook Communication Ministries in Elgin, Illinois. Our trainers included Larry Brook and Susan Miller. Besides all the good stuff they taught us, they reviewed and commented on my first curriculum so that when I got back to Nairobi, I was able to fine-tune it and publish it a few years later. I left that workshop feeling deeply challenged to make a difference through my writing and Sunday school ministry. I later took a distance-learning writing course supervised by Susan Miller that required me to tell stories of my childhood and young formative years. These were later complied into *Chika Goes to School*, a book which aims to encourage girls in their education.

Another encourager I met on my journey was Phoebe Mugo, the managing editor of Uzima Press, Nairobi, in the 1990s. She encouraged me to develop three titles for Uzima Press, which she published under the Books for Life series. Two of the books became bestsellers. She reliably sent me evaluations every year to show me how well my books were doing. That was a booster to my writing career. Margareta of Keswick Bookshop in Nairobi was another great encourager who boosted my morale as a writer. She participated in funding, publishing, and marketing the book *Chika Goes to School*—the story of my quest to excel in school in a culture where girls' education was not very much encouraged.

Last but not least, attending LittWorld 2006 in Brazil, where I participated in a panel discussion, and LittWorld 2012 in Nairobi, where I led workshops and participated in another panel, has boosted my courage. I am now convinced that what I am doing as a writer is an important Kingdom business that is impacting lives all over the world.

How My Christian Faith Influenced My Writing Journey

There is a popular saying that "you can only give what you have". Writing is like giving. Writers give a part of themselves to the readers. The word "Christian" means Christ-like, given that the disciples were called Christians because they looked like or behaved like Jesus Christ. Having received so much grace from God, it is only fair that I share it with other people through my writings.

> For by grace you have been saved through faith, and that not of yourselves; it is the gift of God, not of works, lest anyone should boast (Ephesians 2:8-9, NKJV).

The grace and the unction to write come from above and flow out of my belly "as rivers of living water" (John 7:38). In order for this water not to become stagnant like the water in a lake and begin to stink, I have had to constantly let it flow into other people's lives through my writings. The more I let it flow, the more I get refilled and refreshed for God's glory.

My Christian faith kept me going strong when I faced discouragement and difficulties in my writing career. Many Bible passages were like tonic to my soul. Writing can be a lonely profession because one has to sit in a quiet environment to concentrate better. Most times, this happens when everyone in the family has gone to bed. After the first draft comes the hard task of editing and proofreading to produce something appealing to readers. It is no easy task. It requires a lot of discipline, pain, patience, and perseverance.

A Mandate from Heaven

My happiest moments are when I am crafting a story, a testimony, or an article. I love playing with words while writing and later during editing. Sometimes I feel as if the Holy Spirit is dictating to me what I should write. This helps me know that God is involved in what I am doing. He is the One who gave me the gift of writing, and I am carrying out my destiny by writing, editing, and publishing. I see it as a mandate from heaven. Writing is my first pulpit through which I minister to the whole world and change lives. Praise God for many lives that have been changed or impacted.

My Greatest Joys and Riches

My greatest satisfaction comes when people write to tell me that my books have been a blessing to them. I feel very happy and thankful to God for giving me anointed hands whenever I receive such testimonies from different countries. One that stands out in my mind is a woman in a refugee camp in Kenya (from a different religion) who wept when she read the first chapter of *Growing in Christ When Young*, where I used a vivid story to narrate how God sacrificed his only son for the sins of humanity. I was told she instantly gave her life to Christ.

A lady pastor from Chad wrote to tell me how she got healed after reading my book *Healing from Depression*. She said she was bedridden and almost paralyzed, but after reading how I was healed from depression, she received enough faith and strength to rise up from her sickbed.

A lady named Alice from Senegal said, "I have read all four of your books in French. They have blessed me so much, especially *The Power of Worship*. You seem to have poured out your whole heart in that book. Thank you so much! So when is your next book coming out?"

Her last statement challenged me to write more. My greatest joys and riches are in the lives being impacted positively, in the people receiving encouragement, healing, and guidance through my writings.

Ideas and Inspiration Are Not Sold in the Market

I get inspiration and ideas for writing from four primary sources. The first one is from the Holy Spirit. When the Holy Spirit discovers a vacuum in my life or the lives of those in the church, he begins to lead me to research about that topic. He leads me to read other books and the Scriptures. When my learning is completed and my own life is being impacted, he then tells me to write and share the same thing with other people. That is what happened with the books *Growing in Christ When Young* and *The Power of Worship*. He teaches me first, and then he asks me to teach other people. I thank God for such a privilege.

My second source of ideas and inspiration is publishers. One day the managing editor of Uzima Press asked me, "Can you write us a book about fasting?" It was very easy to say yes because I have practiced fasting all my life, beginning as a young person in secondary school. So *Discipline of Fasting* was written within a short time. Two books followed after that first one.

A third source of ideas is my own life experiences and environment. I wrote an article for a magazine titled *Traffic Jam in Hell* simply because whenever I drove past a particular mortuary in Nairobi, I noticed it was packed with people bringing in or collecting a dead body. I began to imagine how the road to hell must be jammed with people and cars. Also, when I received healing from spiritual attacks and depression, I felt it was a good idea to share the experience so that others going through the same could learn that God can get them out of such circumstances.

My fourth source of ideas is the readers. For instance, when several people told me they could not find good books on prayer, I was motivated to write one to meet the needs of readers.

Obstacles and Frustrations Are Part of the Game

I encountered obstacles right from day one of my writing career. The first obstacle was when someone very close to me told me it would be better to write secular books and novels than Christian books because the latter do not sell well and so would not be a good investment. I pondered over these words for a while and seemed to hear Jesus asking Peter three times, "Do you love me?...Feed my lambs" (John 21:15).

Then I asked myself a few questions like, "Wait a minute, if you do not write for God's Kingdom, who will do it?"

It was as if I heard God asking me as he had asked the Prophet Isaiah, "Whom shall I send and who will go for us?" I was able to answer, "Here am I. Send me" (Isaiah 6:8). I defied the odds and began writing for Christ. What that advisor had told me was true. Not many people like to buy Christian books. Many would rather buy novels and comic books that entertain.

Another obstacle was the inability to find traditional publishers to take on some of my very first manuscripts. That led me to self-publishing, which has more disadvantages than advantages. However, after I had published a few books, some publishers were attracted to my work and began to publish them.

Self-publishing has many challenges and disadvantages. The two major ones are author fatigue and distribution.

In traditional publishing, the in-house editor takes care of the editing and proofreading. But as a self-published author of some of my books, I find it very challenging to do everything from the book conception to the printing. Even after doing peer critique and commissioning an editor to edit the book-in-the-making, the onus still falls on me to read through again and make sure everything is alright before going to press. It is very tiring to go through one document up to five times. Fatigue and loss of interest often sets in, especially if there is no encourager prodding me on to "press towards the goal and obtain the prize" as the Bible says in Philippians 3:14.

While the book is at the press, some follow-up work has to be done—checking the printing quality, the collation, and the trimming to make sure they are all of good quality. After the book is out comes the challenge of marketing and distribution. Only those who have extra funds and moral support can think of launching a book because this can be costly too. Some authors do recover the overhead cost of their book in one day during the launch. This has never been my experience. Scepticism towards self-published books also impacts sales negatively. But the work of the Kingdom of God has to continue through the help of the One who gave the gift.

Perseverance Is the Best Medicine Even in Discouraging Times

"Blessed is the one who perseveres under trial because, having stood the test, that person will receive the crown of life that the Lord has promised to those who love him" (James 1:12, NIV).

The only road that leads to success is perseverance. The sisters to perseverance are called patience and endurance. Character and hope seem to be the grandchildren, and hope does not disappoint. That is how I became qualified to be called an author today. I went through all of those, but I am still looking forward to receiving the crown.

There was a time when I decided to put down my tools and not write anymore. For a year or two, I did not open any of my computer files until I received a few rebukes from the Master, the Creator of heaven and earth. "I know your struggles and pains," I heard God say to me, "but I am the one who gave you the gift for my own glory, so continue writing. Do not focus on the problems and difficulties but focus on me. It is all about me."

I hurriedly picked up my tools and the requisite courage and began to roll out some books again to the joy of my readers. I wouldn't say the difficulties are over now. Difficulties will always be part of our earthly lives. There can be no roses without thorns, but they add spice to our daily lives when the victory comes. God made it so that we might have victories and testimonies to lift up his name. Some people say that tests lead to testimonies. I believe it.

Joan Campbell

South Africa

Joan Campbell lives in Johannesburg, South Africa. She is married to Roy, and they have two daughters. Joan has written for the Upper Room and Scripture Union South Africa. She is the author of *Encounters: Life Changing Moments with Jesus*, a collection of short stories, devotionals, and prayers that transport readers into ancient Israel for personal glimpses of Jesus. Her Christian fantasy series, *The Poison Tree Path Chronicles*, is an allegory that tells the story of humanity's separation from God and Christ's sacrificial death to bring redemption. The first book of the trilogy, *Chains of Gwyndorr*, was a gold medallist in the Young Adult category of the 2017 Illumination Awards.

To overcome her dislike of public speaking, Joan joined Toastmasters in 2016 and is now an active member of her club. Joan enjoys being outdoors, particularly playing tennis, walking her dog, or taking in the beautiful nature and wildlife of South Africa.

To read her blog or find out more about her books and writing, visit: www.joancampbell.co.za.

Gifts On My Writing Journey

On 23 April, 2015 I opened one of the most significant emails of my life. It read, "If you are still waiting, then I would like to make an offer to you to publish with Enclave Publishing."

A publishing contract!

How I had longed for and sought after this. In all the years that I had been working towards this moment, I had believed that the publishing contract—and the ensuing books—were the writer's true treasure. With time and reflection, I now realise that I was mistaken. Don't get me wrong! There's a great joy in sharing one's written words with people and in seeing one's calling to write bear fruit. Yet I now believe that the greater gifts were ones I received on the journey that brought me to this point. A journey that started in my childhood.

I was born in Johannesburg, South Africa, in the 1970s. It was a tumultuous time in my country's history. The struggle against apartheid was brought into tragic focus in places like Sharpeville and Soweto. As the daughter of Dutch immigrants growing up on a flower farm, my life was far removed from these cruel realities. My sister and I grew up running free and wild on the farm, a place where our imaginations could flourish. Every evening we pressed in close to my father's side as he read Dutch fairy tales to us. On the bus ride to school and on the occasional rainy day, we read library books, our mother incentivising this reading by paying us one *rand* (South African money currency) for every book we completed.

So it was that I grew up loving books and words. At about age ten, I would often write poems or short stories. But as my school work increased, these writings dwindled. By the time I was a university student, I hadn't written anything in a long time. Then came the demands of a career and motherhood, also not particularly conducive to creative pursuits.

Yet I felt a growing dissatisfaction. I wanted to write, and with every passing month that I didn't, the desire grew stronger. One of the hurdles that kept me from writing was that I couldn't think of a story to tell. It was at that time when I came across *The Lion, the Witch, and the Wardrobe*. Through C.S. Lewis's writing,

I discovered what a powerful vehicle a story can be for imparting deeper truths. I knew I wanted to do this too. Slowly the seed of an idea began to form—a fantasy story which would tell something of the rift between God and ourselves and how Christ came to bridge it.

So I began to write *The Poison Tree Path*. It took almost three years to complete. Not only was I the mother of two young daughters, but there was a great deal for me to learn about my own writing process, style, and voice. Things like the best time for me to write (late afternoon), whether to plan the plot or just go with the flow (go with the flow), whether to push ahead with the story or edit along the way (push ahead and edit later). Books and online articles could teach me a great deal, but ultimately I had to learn to trust myself too—a very significant lesson.

Imagine my delight when I finally typed "The End". All I had to do now was find a publisher.

I look back and smile at my naivety in thinking it would be that easy. It wasn't. Finding a publisher would prove to be the most challenging and frustrating part of the journey, yet in many ways also the richest and most meaningful. I had learnt a great deal in the writing of the book, but God had many more lessons to teach me in the long years to publication.

One of these lessons came at a one-day conference held by two South African publishing experts. One of them asked the question, "Why do you write?" This is what I wrote in response:

> I write because… it is who I am in the deepest part of me. To not write feels like a betrayal of myself. A stunting. A death.
>
> I write because… it helps me comprehend the world. In describing emotions, I have to dig deep, beyond the superficial level of my own— or another's—heart. To create a scene requires more than a cursory glance; it requires seeing and perceiving, hearing and understanding, tasting and enjoying.
>
> I write because… I long to connect with others. Words are dry when they tumble from my lips. They crack and warp with nervousness. But on a page, my words sing and dance with joy. They come alive, at least for me, which makes me hope they come alive for others too.

I write because… I love to be surprised. I am a wife and mother. I cook, clean, drive, listen, and counsel. My life is full of routine and schedules. Yet the moment I drop into a story, everything changes. I'm somewhere else, and anything can happen. Even as the creator of the story, I am delighted by the twists and turns because often I don't see them coming. For an hour or two each day, I live different and more exciting lives, and the spark of that ignites my own predictable life with joy and purpose too.

I write because…I hope my words will touch and change hearts and lives. Maybe there is something a bit arrogant about this—thinking that I have something to offer the world. Yet I am unable to deny this deep longing, which is the reason why I can't just enjoy writing and then let the manuscript languish in a suitcase under the bed.

In short, I am compelled to write despite the sobering stats and meagre chances of finding a publisher. I write because I am a writer.

This was a significant realisation for me. I am a writer, and therefore I am compelled to write. I knew then that I would keep writing whether I found a publisher or not. The insight was a wonderful and affirming gift.

I continued to send out query letters. Very few publishers responded, but those that did were in agreement—the manuscript was too long. So I began the process of changing my single book into a trilogy.

2012 was a turning point for me. It began with a promise from God. As I read about Joshua and the battle for Jericho, I sensed God whispering into my soul, "I will bring down the walls." I knew instantly that he meant the high publishing walls that I kept battering up against. Walls I just could not breach myself.

2012 was also the year I attended MAI's LittWorld in Kenya. Christian writers, publishers, literary agents, and missionaries from more than fifty nations converged on Limuru for the five-day conference. That first night as we lifted our voices in praise, a shiver ran over me. *This is what heaven will feel like*, I thought. The experience—and the friends I made from every part of the world—has been one of the most precious gifts on my writing journey.

At LittWorld I had the chance to have a one-on-one meeting with British publisher Tony Collins. After grilling me about my manuscript, he agreed to take a look at it. At the end of the week, he had read twelve chapters, and he gave me a note which began, "Joan, you are getting a lot of things right." Then he told me everything I was getting wrong! His advice was pure gold. I went home and did an extensive re-write of my manuscript based on everything Tony suggested I work on. This was another wonderful gift—the time and wisdom of willing mentors.

I will bring down the walls. I could not forget God's promise, but as the years wore on, a part of me began to doubt it. Had I misinterpreted the promise? Perhaps in my great desire to be published, I had only imagined it. Or perhaps God had meant other—maybe emotional or spiritual—walls. Yet even though I occasionally doubted, my spirit did not let go of the promise. I continued to have faith as I leaned on God and learnt to trust him completely with the timing and manner of the promise's fulfilment. God used this time to show me much about the condition of my heart. I had allowed my desire for publication to become an idol in my life, taking that central place that only he should have.

Slowly God began to change my motives. No longer did I want to be a published author to gain acclaim for myself, but rather the desire changed to one of wanting to serve him through my writing. I began to realise that my ability and desire to write came from him. Writing was a calling on my life, but it was not for my own benefit. Rather, it was to be used to grow his Kingdom. What a profoundly beautiful treasure this sense of purpose has become in my life.

I also realised that a time of waiting need not be a barren season. As I waited for God to fulfil his promise, I continued to write, working on completing my trilogy. I also established a blog and experimented with different kinds of writing. I found genuine joy in writing short stories based on encounters Jesus had with people in the gospels. Whenever I shared one of these stories on my blog, a flurry of comments would come in. Readers liked them! They begged me to write more. Eventually I had twenty stories, to which I added a reflection and prayer before self-publishing them in 2014 in a book called *Encounters: Life Changing Moments with Jesus*.

The book has been a blessing in my life and in the lives of others. I still get requests from people asking if they can share one of my stories in a Bible study or church service. I know now that as a writer I need to be faithful in scattering my handful of word-seeds into the wind, allowing God to take them where they need to go. In God's eyes, the "harvest" from the small distribution run of a self-published book is just as meaningful as a book with higher sales figures.

Another gift in this waiting season was the invitation from MAI to become a workshop facilitator in South Africa. I returned to Kenya in 2013 for training, where I met remarkable Christian writers, journalists, and publishers from across Africa. We shared a heart for God to reach Africa through the written word. Yet I returned to South Africa feeling a little out of my depth. I have never been very comfortable with public speaking, and hosting workshops was very far out of my comfort zone. Still, with the help of some remarkable people, I ran a devotional writing workshop in 2014 and a two-day workshop called *My Story for His Glory* in 2015. God also continues to bring young writers into my life, and I try to give them some of the same direction and mentorship that has been so graciously extended to me over the years.

At the point where I had surrendered my writing completely to God, I opened the email from Enclave Publishing offering me a contract for *The Poison Tree Path Chronicles* trilogy. It is difficult to describe the emotions of that moment, but the overriding one was a sense of awe at a God who is faithful to fulfil every one of his promises. That night I followed the example of one of my favourite writers of all time—King David—and penned a psalm of my own:

> *My heart overflows with joy, Lord*
> *And my lips with praise.*
> *You spoke,*
> *And your words did not fall on barren ground.*
> *You promised,*
> *And your vows proved true.*
> *Joan Campbell*
> *Enemy walls towered above me.*
> *My heart quivered with despair.*
> *But you whispered,*
> *And they cracked to their foundations.*

You breathed,
And they crumbled to dust.
Who am I that the Lord of Heaven's armies goes before me?
Who am I that the King of Angel hosts stands by my side?
When I wavered, Your steady hand supported me.
When I fell, Your strong arms lifted me up.
You, O Lord, are faithful
You, O Lord, prove true.
Endless days my lips could praise You
Yet my words would be too few.

The lessons and growth did not end with the signing of a contract. The very thing that I had yearned for all these years turned out to be rather stressful. Worst of all were the deadlines! In all my years of writing, nobody had ever been waiting for me to send them something. I found that the pressure rather inhibited my creativity.

Working with an editor on a comprehensive edit of my first book was probably the most difficult thing I've ever done. Having the flaws of my work so blatantly pointed out to me tapped into all my insecurities. I felt like I had no right to even call myself a writer and that the publisher had made a terrible mistake taking a chance on me. There were times I just wanted to throw in the towel. Again, I had to find solace in God, reminding myself that he believed enough in me and these books to bring down those towering walls. If *he* believed in me, who was I not to? I did my very best (as the dreaded deadline loomed) to address everything my editor asked for, and at the end of the re-writes I could see how much better the book was. I'm glad to say that the re-writes on the second and third book were a lot easier.

Chains of Gwyndorr launched in South Africa on the first of October, 2016, and two weeks later in the United States. *Heirs of Tirragyl* and *Guardian of Ajalon* were released in 2017.

What a journey this has been! The road has not always been smooth. There have been many detours and dark valleys, but there have also been wonderful mountaintop moments. I have learned much about myself, writing, publishing, and God. Through it all, I have gained a deep sense of purpose. I have met the most incredible people on the way, many who stretched out a hand and lifted me to a new place on the road.

Writing has not been an easy calling to follow. Sometimes the disappointment of yet another rejection letter threatened to overwhelm me, and I would cry out to God, "Why did you put this desire in my heart? It's just too difficult!" But he was always there, gently picking me up and putting me back on the road, often using somebody to give me a small word of encouragement to strengthen me. As difficult as the journey has been, I am grateful for every step of it. If I had not taken all those steps, I would not have received the many gifts God had in store for me.

I am a writer. I am compelled to write whether I want to or not. Whether a publisher offers me a contract or not. Whether people applaud my work or not. I am called to write for the glory of God and I am humbled and overjoyed that he has given me this gift and mission.

About Media Associates International (MAI)

Where the global Church is growing, too often a lack of homegrown Christian literature hinders its maturity and outreach. In many nations, less than five percent of the available Christian content is written by local authors. To help combat this famine of Christian literature, Media Associates International (MAI) equips men and women to create life-transforming books and articles in their heart language.

Since our founding in 1985, we have conducted training in more than 85 countries for 9,500 participants. As a result, we have seen budding writers developed, publishing houses grown, periodicals launched, and books produced.

Our ministry has grown through our global network of trainers, now numbering more than 50 active volunteer trainers. These Christian publishing professionals make themselves available to equip others in their respective areas of the world.

MAI regional Trustees in Asia, Africa, and Europe spearhead training in their respective areas and offer valuable input for our international **programme**.

Our training is rooted in the conviction that God uses the written word to transform lives. We also believe a vibrant body of indigenous Christian literature is essential to the strength and vitality of the Church.

We conduct an average of at least one in-country training per month somewhere in the world. Plus, we hold the triennial LittWorld conferences. As an outcome of our LittWorld conferences in Kenya in 2009 and 2012, the MAI-Africa Trustees group came into being. The Africa Trustees spearhead our publishing and writer training on the continent.

We are responding to increased opportunities for helping global publishers and writers create excellent content that enriches the Church and influences society.

MAI seeks to strengthen and develop robust and financially self-sustaining Christian publishers who will publish excellent content by local authors. It is our prayer that this book will help inspire and equip a new generation of Christian authors across Africa.

For more information about MAI, please visit our website: littworld.org

---

MAI-Africa

As a part of the Media Associates International, MAI-Africa spearheads writer and publisher training for the African continent. This trustees' group was launched after LittWorld 2012 in Nairobi, Kenya.

Contact MAI-Africa

mai-africa@littworld.org
PO Box 30446-00100
Nairobi, Kenya

Trustees

Rose Birenge
Chair, Biblica Africa, Kenya

Nelson Clemens
Consultant, Sierra Leone

Lawrence Darmani
Step Publishers, Ghana

Joanna Ilboudo
ACTS, Burkina Faso

Dr. Kirimi Barine
Publishing Consultant, Kenya

Lekan Otufodunrin
Online Editor, The Nation, Nigeria

Jules Ouoba
CPE Publishing House, Côte d'Ivoire

Kingston Ogango
Alpha International, Kenya

Printed and bound by PG in the USA